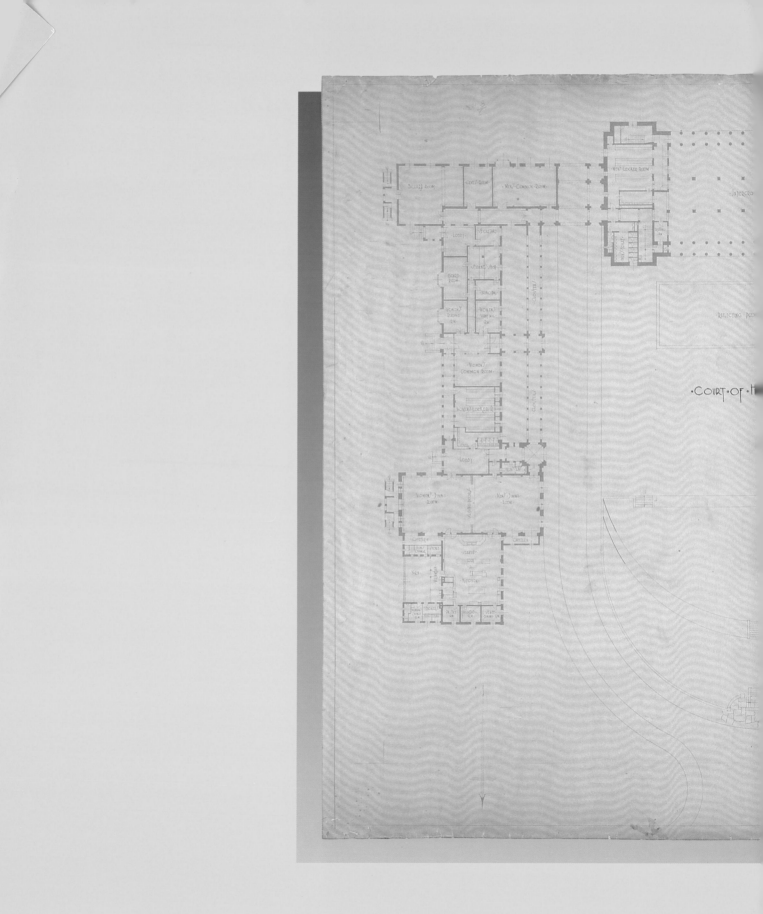

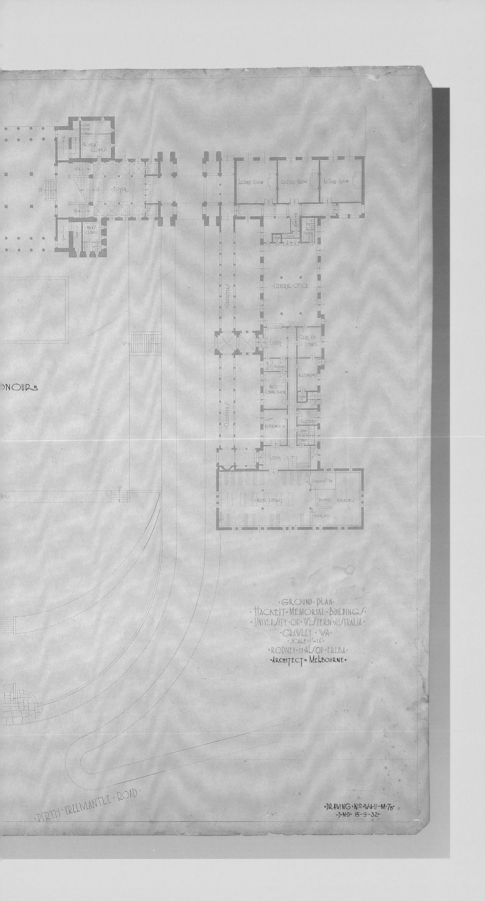

·GROUND·PLAN·
·HACKETT·MEMORIAL·BUILDINGS·
·UNIVERSITY·OF·WESTERN·AUSTRALIA·
·CRAWLEY·W·A·
·SCALE·1"=16'·
·RODNEY·H·ALSOP·F·R·I·B·A·
·ARCHITECT·MELBOURNE·

·PERTH·FREEMANTLE·ROAD·

·DRAWING·No·N·W·I·U·M·76·
·D·M·D·15-9-32·

CRAWLEY CAMPUS

This first edition is limited to
1,000 deluxe soft cover copies, individually numbered
and signed by the author.

This is copy number __198__

Great Gate, Winthrop Hall

CRAWLEY CAMPUS

The Planning And Architecture Of The University Of Western Australia

R. J. Ferguson

UNIVERSITY OF WESTERN AUSTRALIA PRESS

First published in 1993 by
University of Western Australia Press
Nedlands, Western Australia, 6009

National Library of Australia
Cataloguing-in-Publication entry:

Ferguson, R.J. (Ronald Jack), 1931–
     Crawley campus: the planning and architecture of The University of Western
     Australia.

     Bibliography.
     Includes index.
     ISBN 1 875560 27 0.

     1. University of Western Australia – Buildings. 2.
     Universities and colleges – Western Australia – Crawley –
     Design and construction. 3. Campus planning – Western
     Australia – Crawley. 4. College buildings – Western
     Australia – Crawley – Design and plans. I. Title

727.3099411

Consultant Editor Amanda Curtin, Curtin Communications, Perth
Design by Susan Eve Ellvey, Designpoint, Perth
Typeset in Galliard by Scott Four Colour Print, Perth
Printed by Scott Four Colour Print, Perth

FOREWORD

The Crawley campus at The University of Western Australia is one of the most beautiful in the world. The foundation for this beauty is the wonderful riverside location, which was granted with great foresight by the Government of the time, for Western Australia's first university.

This early good fortune has been consistently used to excellent purpose, both in the buildings which grace the site and in its landscaping.

Great care has been taken since the University's earliest days to look to the long term and to plan for the entirety of the University's lands. We see this still today, where the southern part of the campus is now being developed in a way that remains consistent with the early plans. It seems likely that there is a connection between this consistency and the undoubted quality of those early plans as well as the degree of consensus they achieved.

An international competition was used to find designs for the principal University buildings – the Hackett Memorial Buildings, of which Winthrop Hall is the centrepiece. This search for the best set the tone for the future.

This book ably documents and illustrates the history of the Crawley campus from the viewpoint of its buildings, and the plans that led to their construction. It is a history of creativity and conservation, and it is particularly appropriate that it is the work of Mr Gus Ferguson, one of those architects to whom the University is so indebted for the sensitive development of its campus.

Publication of *Crawley Campus* brings to the wider public a selection of the great store of architectural drawings, plans and photographs that have been so carefully preserved as part of the University's history. It tells the story of how well the University has been served by its decision-makers, its planners and architects who have been able to build on early brilliance, to follow and improve on this, and have created the tranquil, harmonious campus to be seen today.

Professor Fay Gale
Vice-Chancellor, The University of Western Australia

ACKNOWLEDGMENTS

Much of the historical detail which accompanies the illustrations in this publication was taken from Professor Fred Alexander's *Campus at Crawley A Narrative and Critical Appreciation of the First Fifty Years of The University of Western Australia*, published in 1963. The writer is indebted to the research and source material contained in *Campus at Crawley* and grateful for Emeritus Professor Alexander's permission to quote so freely from his work.

Many of the illustrations depicted herein were taken from archival material which had been catalogued for the University by Barbara van Bronswijk, who was generous in supplying information from her own research.

The efforts of the University Archivist Christine Bapty and Records Officer Jennifer Edgecombe in finding and making available University records and illustrations are much appreciated.

Thanks are due to Colin Murphy and Roger Webber of Media Services for photographing the original illustrations, some of which were in worse than fragile condition; to Jennifer Harvey and Lynnette Gardiner for their assistance in researching and preparing text and illustrations; and to Joslyn Boulay for typing the manuscript.

CONTENTS

INTRODUCTION

The physical development of the Crawley campus of The University of Western Australia was initiated in 1914. In this year, the State Government made available to the University a 104 acre (42 hectare) site adjacent to Matilda Bay on the Swan River, and the Department of Mining and Engineering moved from the University's temporary home in Irwin Street in the Perth city centre to the new site to occupy the homestead which had been constructed there around 1846.

A competition for the planning of the campus was conducted late in 1914, and the University's first new building was constructed at the north-eastern corner of the campus in 1923 to provide accommodation for the departments of Biology and Geology.

The foundation Chancellor of the University, the Hon. Sir John Winthrop Hackett, died in 1916, leaving many bequests. One was a provision for the construction of a 'Great Hall' and facilities for Administration and Students to designs to be selected from an architectural competition, which was eventually conducted in 1926. Another bequest became available in 1926 for the construction of the first student residential accommodation on campus.

The foundation Professor of Architecture at Sydney University, Leslie Wilkinson, was commissioned in 1926 to advise on a campus planning review and also to assist in the conduct of the architectural competition for the University's memorial buildings.

The University has in its archives many of the drawings of this early period of the physical development of the campus, including illustrations from the architectural competition and the design and development of buildings and campus plans thereafter. Most of the fragile drawings have been catalogued and encapsulated for their protection but, being archival material, are relatively difficult to access.

This book presents some of the many illustrations created in the pursuit of the optimum layout and design of the University's buildings which, together with its landscaping, contribute to the making of one of Australia's finest university campuses.

FOUNDATION

The first definite step towards a university in Western Australia was taken in 1898 when the Adelaide University Extension Committee was formed. The Committee arranged for visits to Perth from lecturers and, with the co-operation of the University of Adelaide, public and university degree examinations were held.[1] The extension lecture service played a significant part in the education of Western Australians on the nature and importance of a university. Lectures in Perth were well attended, and country centres were also visited. Lecturers were recruited from other Australian universities and from as far afield as the United Kingdom.[2]

In 1904, the Parliament of Western Australia passed the University Endowment Act whereby about 4,000 acres (1,620 hectares), mostly of suburban lands, were set aside as an endowment for a future university. In 1909, a Royal Commission chaired by John Winthrop Hackett was appointed to report on whether the time was ripe for the establishment of a university, and, if so, what type of university it should be.[3]

The Royal Commission urged immediate action. Taking population, revenue and national development into account and comparing conditions in the State – 'the only considerable member of the white dominions of the Crown without a University' – with those which had operated elsewhere in Australia when universities had been founded, it declared that the argument for the immediate establishment of a university stood 'practically without answer'.[4]

The University of Western Australia Act was passed in 1911, and in the following year the first Senate was appointed. This consisted of eighteen members, with Hackett as Chancellor. Of the eight foundation chairs filled early in 1913, two belonged to the Faculty of Arts – English, and History and Economics; four were classed as pure science – Biology, Chemistry, Geology, and Mathematics and Physics; and two were in applied science – Agriculture, and Mining and Engineering.[5]

Hackett, as chairman of the Royal Commission, observed that 'in the care of our own State the University must be in no sense provincial but national in the fullest and most pregnant meaning of the word'.[6]

The new institution was to be a University of Western Australia and not just a University of Perth.

At a meeting on 17 August 1936, the Senate resolved 'that the date of the foundation of the University should be regarded as 13 February 1912...', this being the date of the constitution of the first Senate.[7]

REFERENCES

1. *Opening of Winthrop Hall, Commemoration Volume and Official Programme*, p. 6.
2. F. Alexander, *Campus at Crawley*, p. 23.
3. *Opening of Winthrop Hall, Commemoration Volume and Official Programme*, p. 6.
4. F. Alexander, *Campus at Crawley*, p. 26.
5. *Opening of Winthrop Hall, Commemoration Volume and Official Programme*, p. 6.
6. F. Alexander, *Campus at Crawley*, p. 27.
7. *Senate Minutes*, 17 August 1936.

Temporary Accommodation

The newly founded University rented temporary administrative offices from the Church of England in Cathedral Chambers, Cathedral Avenue, in the centre of the city, from May 1912 until 1916. These offices were only a short distance from the site of the University's first, but temporary, teaching facilities.

Later in 1912, after exploring other locations including the Observatory site behind Parliament House and a site on the corner of Bazaar Terrace and William Street, the State Government made available to the University a 1.1 acre (0.45 hectare) site on the immediate west side of Irwin Street, with frontages to both St Georges Terrace and Hay Street.

The first building erected on this site was designed by the Public Works Department and constructed of timber framing with weatherboard wall cladding and corrugated iron roof sheeting. It was completed by the beginning of the academic year in 1913 and provided accommodation for both teaching and administration until joined by other buildings on the site.[1] The building fronted St Georges Terrace and measured 110 feet (33.5 metres) long by 20 feet (6.1 metres) wide. Its 7 feet (2.1 metres) wide verandah facing St Georges Terrace was enclosed in about 1918 to provide additional accommodation. The whole structure, with others, was transported late in 1932 to the Crawley site, where it served many purposes until being rescued from demolition in 1987. It was then 'restored' and relocated to the west side of James Oval where it currently (1993) provides accommodation for Convocation and is also used as a cricket pavilion. It is known as the 'Irwin Street Building'.

Additional accommodation at Irwin Street, provided in lightweight structures, was obtained from other, sometimes remote, locations. The Workers' Hall transported from Coolgardie in 1917 was employed as the administration office of the University.[2] Other buildings, including the Oddfellows Hall relocated from Oxford Street, Leederville, and two buildings from the Pensioners Barracks formerly used by the State Brick Works and the State Sawmills, provided accommodation for a women's club in 1917 and a library in 1927.[3]

The location was known simply as Irwin Street or, because of the metal clad buildings, more affectionately as 'Tin Pan Alley' – some say 'Tin Pot Alley'.

The Perth Technical College had opened to students in 1900, the Teachers Training College at Claremont in 1902 and the School of Mines at Coolgardie in 1902, expanding to Kalgoorlie in 1903. The agricultural college at Muresk opened in 1926.[4]

REFERENCES

1. F. Alexander, *Campus at Crawley*, p. 62.
2. ibid.
3. Public Works Department plan folder PWD 18942, Battye Library.
4. F. Alexander, *Campus at Crawley*, p. 6.

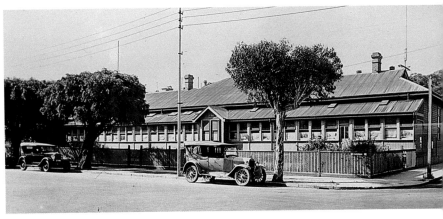

*Administration building, Irwin
Street, circa 1920s*

*First building constructed at Irwin
Street, 1913*

Plan, Irwin Street site, circa 1920s

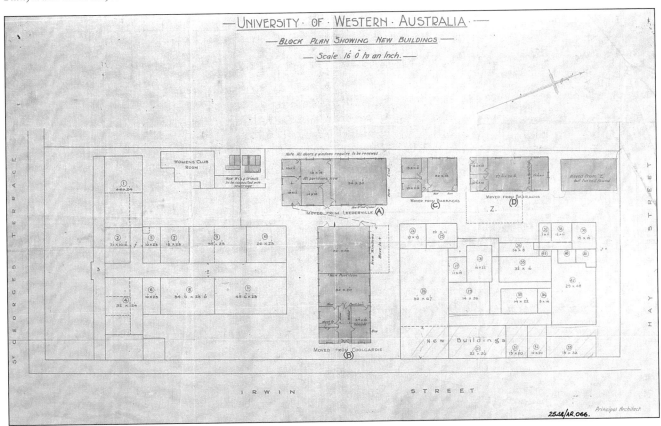

ST JOHN'S UNIVERSITY HOSTEL

The University's first residential hostel was located in a building at the western end of St Georges Terrace within easy walking distance of the University's temporary location at Irwin Street.

In June 1858, Perth's first Anglican Bishop, Mathew Blagden Hale, opened a boys secondary school in a house on a 2 acre (0.81 hectare) site Hale had purchased privately and which had frontages to both Hay Street and St Georges Terrace opposite Mill Street. In 1862, the English Society for Promoting Christian Knowledge contributed towards the cost of a new building for 'the Church of England Collegiate School' on the same site, and the eastern wing of what became known as 'the cloisters' was constructed.[1] The school became known as the 'Bishop's School' and also 'Bishop Hale's School'.

The 'Bishop's School' operated in the building until 1877 when it moved to a new secular day school established by the Government. This high school became known as Hale School.

'The cloisters' building was used as a boarding-house for high school and theological students until 1879, when it was used as a girls school founded by Bishop Hutton Parry.[2] Additions were made in two stages in 1879 and 1881 when the western wing was completed. The girls school closed in 1888 and the building was sub-divided and leased by the Church as two private houses until 1900, when the eastern wing became a boarding-house named 'The Cloisters' and the western wing was used as a clergy training college. The building was named St John's College in 1909. By 1918, the college had become a boarding-house for university students and in 1921 was officially recognized as St John's University Hostel.[3] The hostel was closed in 1930 with the imminent move of the University to its permanent home and the construction of St George's College on the Crawley site.

REFERENCES

1. C.E.S. Davis, 'St John's University Hostel', unpublished paper, Battye Library.
2. A.E. Williams, *Western Australia. An Architectural Heritage*, pp. 61-63.
3. C.E.S. Davis, 'St John's University Hostel', unpublished paper, Battye Library.

Cloisters building, circa 1920s

PERMANENT SITE

In 1832, a 32 acre (12.96 hectare) lot, Location 87, fronting what was later called Matilda Bay, was granted to Captain Mark John Currie, RN, in response to his 1829 application to the Surveyor-General, J.S. Roe, for a 'Villa grant in the Bay below Mount Eliza (when that part of the country becomes open for location) about the spot where my tent at present stands'. Currie farmed the property for a short time before returning to the Royal Navy, from which he retired with the rank of Admiral.

Henry C. Sutherland, who had arrived in the Swan River Colony with Currie in 1829, acquired the Currie farm in 1832. Sutherland had held the office of Assistant Surveyor until 1830, when he became Clerk to the Colonial Treasurer and eventually Colonial Treasurer and Collector of Inland Revenue.

Sutherland constructed a two-storey brick homestead around 1846 and developed the property, which he named Crawley Park in memory of his mother, Ann Crawley. Brothers James and Richard Gallop were among those engaged to manage the farm at various times. James later developed his own property nearby and constructed what is now known as Gallop House. After Sutherland's death in 1855, the farm was leased to Frederick Barlee, the Colonial Secretary, until some of the Sutherland family reoccupied the house between around 1860 and 1875, when the property was sold to George Shenton junior.

Shenton, who was born in Perth, became a member of the Legislative Council in 1870 and in 1875 purchased four lots, including Location 87, on Matilda Bay, in the same year occupying the two-storey homestead constructed by Sutherland.

'Rotton' map, 1883

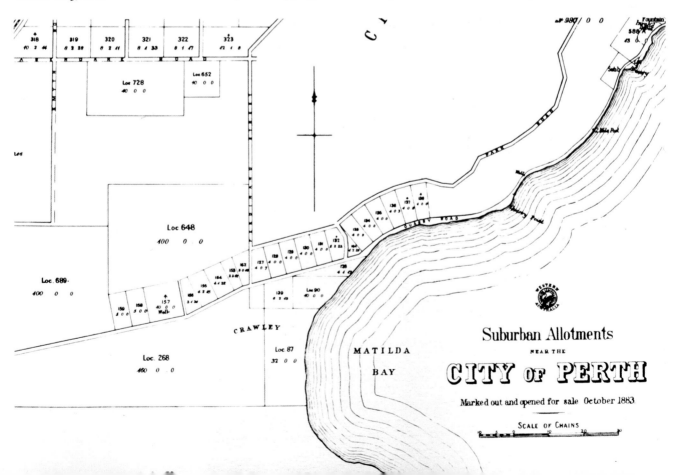

5

In 1871, Shenton was elected to the Perth City Council, acting as Chairman from 1875 to 1877 and as Mayor from 1880 to 1884 and again from 1886 to 1888. During 1892, he was elected President of the Legislative Council and was knighted in 1893. By 1892, Shenton had acquired two other properties on Matilda Bay, increasing the area of his holding to 152 acres (61.56 hectares). After Shenton's death in 1909, the Government, in order to protect access to the river foreshores, resumed the Crawley estate to be used for public purposes.

By 1912, continuing debate regarding the choice of a permanent location for the University had narrowed the field down to three sites: Crawley, Parliament House and West Subiaco. The Crawley estate, which became known as Shenton estate, favoured by many because of its superb river aspects and area in excess of 100 acres (40.5 hectares), was considered by some to be too remote from the city of Perth and others were concerned by its high water-table being close to river level.[1]

The Parliament House site was only 45 acres (18.2 hectares) in area and at that time already accommodated the Observatory, the high school (later Hale School) and the Public Works Department in the old Pensioners Barracks building. This site would have provided instant, but not suitable, accommodation for the University and would have required alternative facilities for those displaced. The site's main appeal was its proximity to the city.[2]

It is notable that during the debate on locating the new Parliament House in 1897, the site at the rear of the Barracks building was thought to be too far removed from the city centre, being 1,440 yards (1.3 kilometres) from the General Post Office.[3]

The site described as West Subiaco (Shenton Park), although of adequate area, had no aspect and its proximity to an 'Asylum for the Insane', a sewage treatment plant, an Infectious Diseases Hospital and a Home for Lost Dogs found few supporters.[4]

The battle of the sites flared again late in 1913, with some proponents favouring a 50 acre (20.25 hectare) site in Kings Park on the corner of Kings Park Road and Thomas Street. The apparent attraction of the Kings Park location was its proximity to the Hay Street tramway and consequently to Perth city.[5]

Fortunately for the University, the debate over its permanent location was settled early in 1914 when the Government made available to the University 104 acres (42.12 hectares) of the Crawley estate, retaining 48 acres (19.44 hectares) for use as a public park.[6] In the same year, the Department of Mining and Engineering moved from Irwin Street to occupy the Shenton homestead. It was not until March 1920 that the University formalized its 999 year lease for the site with the Crown.[7]

REFERENCES

1. R. Stephens, 'A Sweet Spot in an Old Colonial Garden', *Journal and Proceedings of the Royal Western Australian Historical Society*, vol. IV, no. 2. pp. 37-43.
2. F. Alexander, *Campus at Crawley*, p. 63.
3. R.J. Ferguson & Associates, *Parliament House Precinct Policy Review*, p. 6.
4. F. Alexander, *Campus at Crawley*, p. 63.
5. ibid., p. 85.
6. ibid., p. 64.
7. R.J. Ferguson & Associates, *Campus Planning Review 1990*, p. 11.

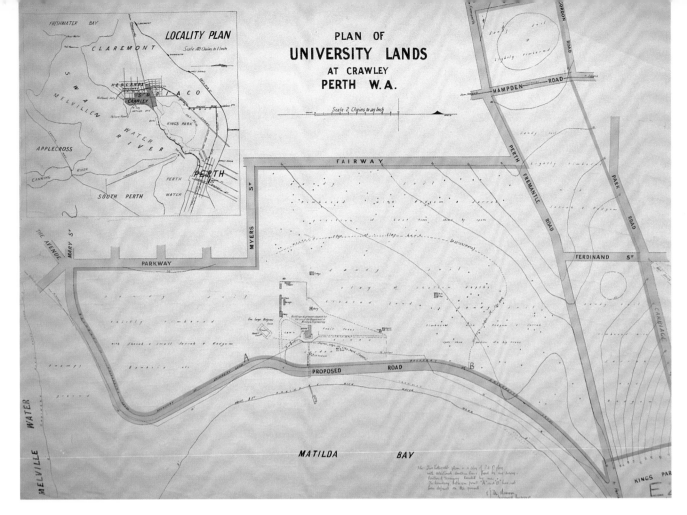

*Plan of University lands at Crawley,
1912*

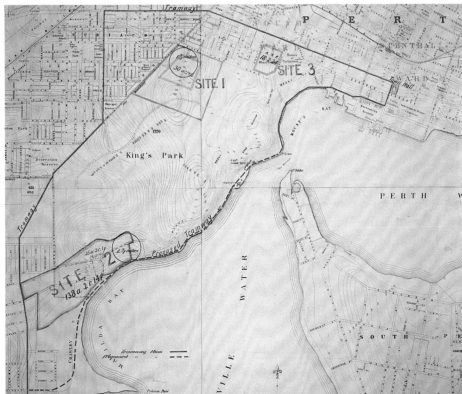

*Alternative sites, Kings Park, circa
1913*

LAYOUT COMPETITION

Despite the period of limited academic growth in the war years of 1914 to 1918 and the inevitable drain on staff and students, positive steps were taken which would lead to the successful development of the Crawley campus.

At a meeting of the Senate in November 1914, the foundation Chancellor, John Winthrop Hackett, announced that he desired to offer two prizes – one of 100 guineas and a second of 25 guineas – for the best suggestions or plan for laying out the Crawley site for University purposes.[1]

A Senate committee of six prepared competition conditions, which were approved by the Building Committee on 4 December 1914.

The requirements included in the 'Particulars for Guidance in the Preparation of Competitive Designs' defined a 'Central Group of Buildings', which became the subject of a competition in 1926, as well as facilities for the different academic departments, a medical school, residential colleges, residences for professors and attendants, and also sporting facilities including a boatshed on the river.

'Approaches' to the site were indicated to be 'either from the east by water, from the west by the Nedlands tram, or from the north-east by the Mounts Bay Road tram. The main Perth Fremantle Road runs through the University Lands...'[2]

Entries were received from Australia, Great Britain, the United States of America and South Africa. On 29 June 1915, the six-member Board of Adjudicators, which included the Chief Government Architect, Hillson Beasley, shortlisted six entries from the twenty-six received and, after further shortlisting, awarded first prize to H. Desbrowe-Annear, a Melbourne architect, and second prize to H.W. Hargrave, a Perth architect. An honourable mention was awarded to J. Cheal and Sons Ltd, 'landscape gardeners' of Crawley, England.[3]

The Senate received the Adjudicators' Report at a meeting on 19 July 1915, agreeing to the awarding of the prizes, and at the same meeting resolved:

(i) That the Building Committee with the addition of the Chief Government Architect should be asked to prepare a plan in consultation with the teaching staff. This plan to be submitted to Senate.

(ii) That the public be allowed to inspect the designs...[4]

This resolution indicated either that there was some disappointment with the result or that it was indeed a competition for ideas which were meant to be developed by others.

Harold Desbrowe-Annear has been described as one of Australia's first 'Functionalist Architects', his name being linked with pioneers such as Hardy Wilson, Robin Dods and Walter Burley Griffin. Desbrowe-Annear worked almost exclusively on houses which were austere in form but with every detail determined by utilitarian purpose. In 1914, he edited a magazine, *For Every Man His Home*. According to Freeland, he had an inventive turn of mind and a belief in the supremacy of reason.[5]

Desbrowe-Annear died in 1933 at the age of 67.

REFERENCES

1. *Senate Minutes*, 16 November 1914.
2. *Information, Conditions and Particulars for Guidance in the Preparation of Competitive Designs for the Laying Out of the Grounds and Gardens including the Disposition of the Buildings of The University of Western Australia*.
3. *Senate Minutes*, 19 July 1915.
4. ibid.
5. J.M. Freeland, *Architecture in Australia a History*, pp. 238-243.

DESBROWE-ANNEAR PLAN

Desbrowe-Annear's plan was based on a system of axes radiating from a point centred on an extension of Ferdinand Street. The main group of buildings, including the Great Hall and accommodation for Administration, Science, Arts and Law, was concentrated on the highest part of the site adjacent to the intersection of Fairway and the Perth Fremantle Road.

It is assumed that the main campus entrance was intended to be from this intersection on what was shown as the Main Axis, terminating at its north-western end on a residential college across the Perth Fremantle Road and at its south-eastern end by a jetty on Matilda Bay across a 'Proposed Road' – now Hackett Drive.

The sparsity of buildings on the eastern and southern areas of the campus did not complement the formality of the internal road system, which cut the site into small segments and may have resulted from fears of river flooding – one of the criticisms of the location during the long site selection debates.

Five residential colleges were located on the north side of the Perth Fremantle Road, as were a group of professors' houses in the north-east corner and a practice oval for the colleges west of Hampden Road on a site eventually to accommodate the Nedlands Teachers Training College.

The plan showed the Shenton homestead maintained in isolation, and provided a site for a Guild building adjacent to the intersection of Ferdinand Street and the Perth Fremantle Road. Tennis courts were located on Myers Street and also adjacent to the Hampden Road practice oval.

First prize design, H. Desbrowe-Annear, 1915

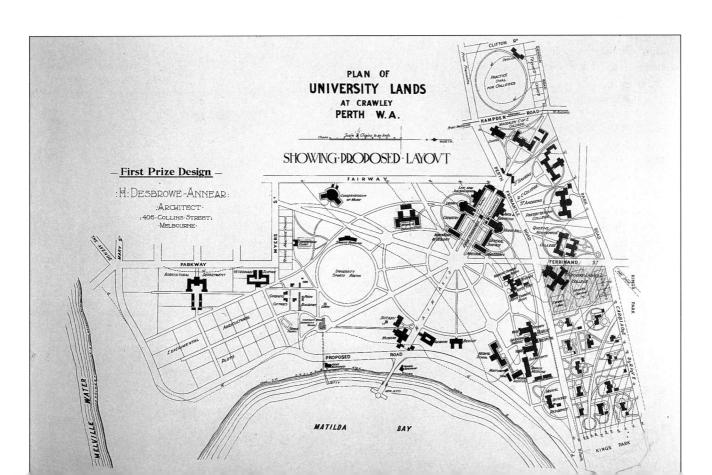

9

Desbrowe-Annear's plan was to suffer criticism and redesign in later years, but some elements of the plan were retained. These include the location of the residential colleges on the north side of Stirling Highway and Mounts Bay Road, the main sports oval, now James Oval, and one north-east axis which was shown as an 'Alley' on the 1927 Wilkinson plan and as Battye Avenue on the 1954-55 Stephenson plan, and which set the orientation of Somerville Auditorium and the Music building.

In 1922, the Senate, in considering recommendations for the science departments to be moved from Irwin Street to the Crawley site, appointed a committee consisting of Vice-Chancellor Whitfeld and architects Sir Talbot Hobbs, W.B. Hardwick and A.R.L. Wright to report on the buildings required and their proposed location on the campus.[1]

The committee's report raised again the old criticisms of the Crawley site and its suitability for building, and in consequence found fault with Desbrowe-Annear's plan. Because of some disagreement between Whitfeld and his architect colleagues regarding building on the low-lying areas of the campus and the cost of building on the higher sloping ground north of the Perth Fremantle Road, the Senate referred the problem to the heads of departments.

The recommendations made by the heads of departments included deleting the provision for professors' houses and constructing accommodation for science departments in their place, commencing with a building for Biology and Geology. The heads of departments' report was accepted by the Senate at a meeting on 21 August 1922, and the Government was requested to provide a building for Biology and Geology on the north-east corner of the campus.[2]

The Public Works Department produced several versions of the Desbrowe-Annear plan, one dated 13 November 1922 showing provisions for science buildings north of Mounts Bay Road but with the main group of buildings centred on the Ferdinand Street axis, which may have influenced the structure of the Wilkinson plan which was to follow. Another, dated 3 September 1923, showed the Biology and Geology building in its built location but with the main group of buildings on the north-west axis. The 1923 version showed Agriculture also north of Mounts Bay Road.

Public Works Department variation of Desbrowe-Annear plan, 1922 ▷

Public Works Department variation of Desbrowe-Annear plan, 1923 ▷

REFERENCES

1. *Senate Minutes*, 15 May 1922.
2. *Senate Minutes*, 21 August 1922.

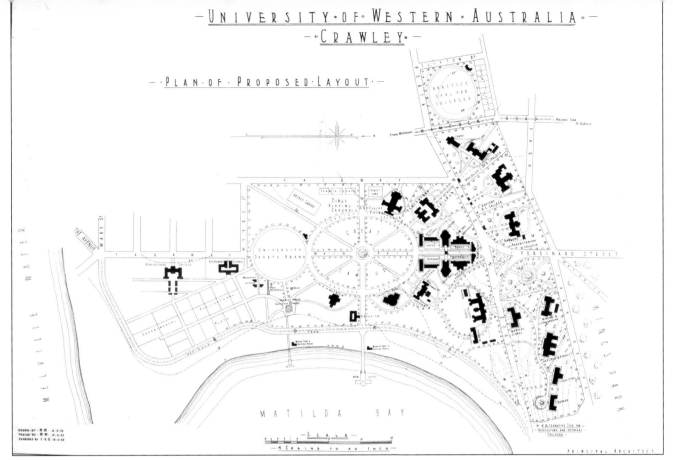

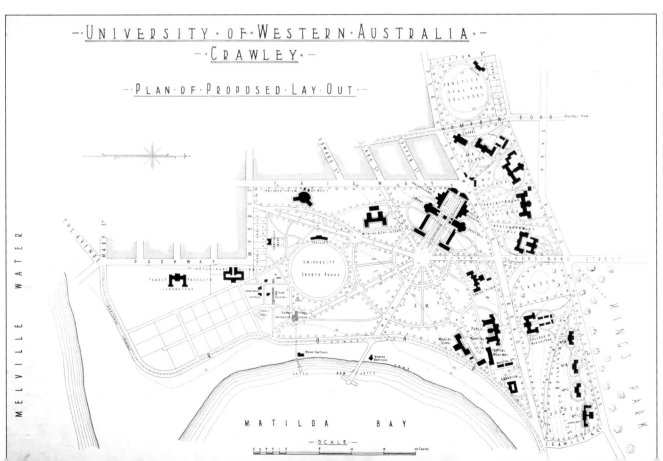

11

BIOLOGY AND GEOLOGY BUILDING

Early in 1923, the Government provided funds for the construction of facilities for Biology and Geology, to be designed by the Public Works Department, William Hardwick being Government Architect at the time.

The first permanent building constructed for the University was basically a two-storey structure linked to a single-storey lecture theatre with service facilities. The building was constructed of red brick walling with Donnybrook stone dressings and terracotta tiled roofs. The neo-Georgian styled building boasts east, west and south columned porches in imposing elevations and a decorative stone flèche on the roof. The east porch served as an entrance to Biology, the west Geology, and the south the Geology teaching and collection laboratory.

The Premier, James Mitchell, officiated at the laying of the foundation stone on 1 September 1923, and the building was completed for occupation at the beginning of the 1925 academic year.[1]

During a Senate inspection of the completed building, the professors of the two occupying departments expressed great dissatisfaction with what they saw as a complete disregard for their departments' requirements, which had been communicated to the Public Works Department in 1923. They were particularly critical of the 'perfectly useless but very expensive stone belfry [flèche] which projects through the roof and requires for its support stone pillars down through the two main laboratories'.[2]

A part single, part two-storey extension was completed in 1945 by the Public Works Department.[3] At a meeting on 20 October 1947, the Senate decided that the Chair of Biology should thereafter be known as Zoology.[4]

Geology remained in this location until 1962, when the department moved to the northern end of the building constructed for Physics and Chemistry in 1935 and which became known as the Geology and Geography building.

REFERENCES

1. F. Alexander, *Campus at Crawley*, p. 116.
2. W. Somerville, 'A Blacksmith Looks at a University', unpublished manuscript, Battye Library, vol. 2, p. 476.
3. *Senate Minutes*, 15 October 1945, Vice-Chancellor's Report.
4. *Senate Minutes*, 20 October 1947.

Biology and Geology building, detail of front porch, 1923 ▷

Biology and Geology building, flèche detail, 1923 ▷

Biology and Geology building, south elevation, 1923

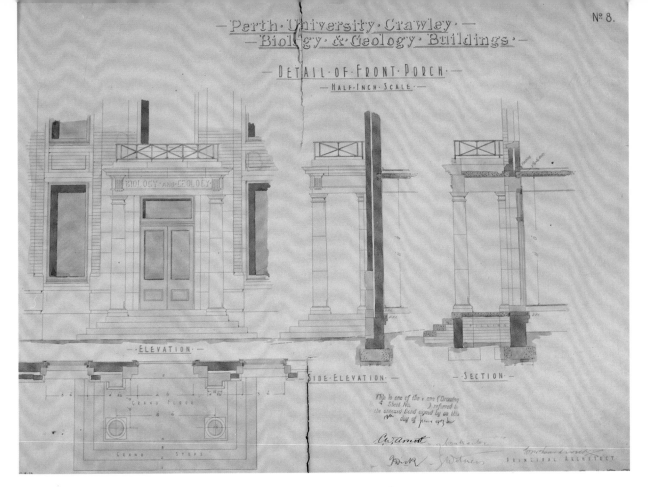

Perth·University·Crawley·
Biology·&·Geology·Buildings·

Detail·of·Front·Porch·
·Half·Inch·Scale·

BIOLOGY AND GEOLOGY

—ELEVATION—

—SIDE·ELEVATION—   —SECTION—

GRAND FLOOR

GRAND STEPS·

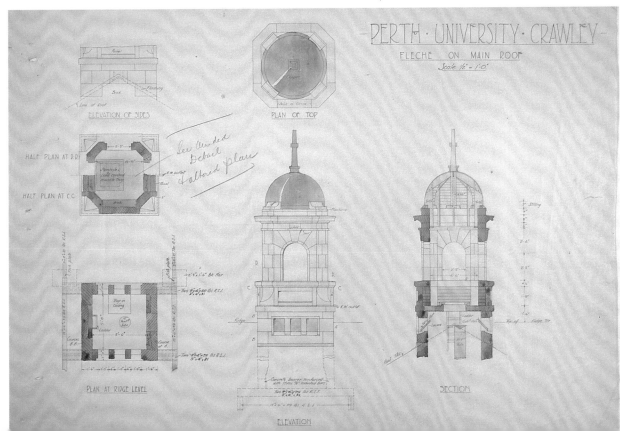

PERTH·UNIVERSITY·CRAWLEY·

FLECHE ON MAIN ROOF

Scale 1/2" = 1'0"

ELEVATION OF SIDES

PLAN OF TOP

HALF PLAN AT D.D.

See Amended
Detail
of altered plan

HALF PLAN AT C.C.

PLAN AT RIDGE LEVEL   ELEVATION   SECTION

13

John Winthrop Hackett

The Hackett Memorial Buildings, which form the centrepiece of the Crawley campus today, are a fitting tribute to the efforts of the University's first Chancellor, John Winthrop Hackett, not only for the bequest which made the construction of these buildings possible but for his dedication to the creation of a university in Western Australia and his contribution to the successful development of the University.

Hackett, born in Lordello, County Dublin, in 1848, graduated from Trinity College in Dublin. He practised law in Sydney for a short time and in 1876 moved to Melbourne, where he became Vice-Principal and then Sub-Warden of Trinity College at Melbourne University where he tutored. He also ventured into journalism to supplement his income. In 1882, he abandoned his academic career to take up a pastoral lease near Carnarvon in Western Australia. During this ill-fated venture, Hackett met Charles Harper, the proprietor of the *West Australian* newspaper. Hackett was offered, and accepted, a partnership in the newspaper, becoming editor in 1887. Sir Charles Harper died in 1912 and Hackett became the sole proprietor of the newspaper.[1]

Hackett's distinction as a journalist was matched by that as a public figure. He was elected to the first Legislative Council in 1893 where he remained for sixteen years. He was a member and became Chairman of the Board of the first Perth High School, was Registrar of the Anglican diocese of Perth and first Chancellor of its Cathedral Church of St George. He was appointed Chairman of the Karrakatta Cemetery Board in 1899 and retained that office until he died in 1916. He pressured for the construction of permanent accommodation for a Public Library, Museum and Art Gallery. He was responsible for the development of the Zoological Gardens in South Perth and participated in the design of Queens Gardens in East Perth. He was Grand Master of the Order of Freemasons between 1901 and 1903.

Hackett's overriding aim was for the establishment of a university in Western Australia and he was the prime instigator of the passing of the University of Western Australia Act in 1911.

Hackett was offered a Knight Bachelorship in 1902, which honour he declined, but accepted a knighthood in 1911 and was created KCMG in 1913. He was married for the first time in 1905, at the age of 57, to Deborah Drake-Brockman, then 17 years old. Hackett died in 1916 at the age of 68 leaving four daughters and a son and making The University of Western Australia and the Church of England his main residuary legatees.[2]

In 1926, while the University was negotiating for additional buildings for Physics and Chemistry which were still accommodated at Irwin Street, and for Mining and Engineering which had occupied the Shenton homestead in 1914, the benefits of the Hackett bequest became known.

When Hackett died in 1916, property values had been depressed by the war and it seemed unlikely that the estate could pay all the bequests set out in his will or that the University and the Church of England would derive any benefit from their positions as residuary legatees.[3] Hackett's will required that his estate be managed by his executors for a period of ten years before being made available to its beneficiaries. By careful management, the other legatees were able to be paid off, and in 1926 the University and Church were informed that the residuary estate comprised the *West Australian* newspaper. The newspaper was sold and the University's share capitalized at £425,000, while the Church received about £140,000.[4]

The bequest in favour of the University made available a sum of £150,000 for the erection of a ceremonial hall (including administrative offices and temporary accommodation for the Library and Faculty of Arts) and a Students' Union building. An endowment of £190,000 was arranged for studentships and bursaries, and two additional endowments provided £10,000 as a students' loan fund and £25,000 to meet in whole or in part the salary of a permanent full-time Vice-Chancellor. An additional sum of £50,000 was set aside as an endowment for the maintenance and management of the buildings and adjoining grounds.[5] The terms of the will required that the designers of the group of ceremonial buildings be selected by means of an open architectural competition and that

> ...considering the importance of fine buildings in the education and refinement of the citizens of a State I direct that...this sum shall be expended by the Senate in the erection of a University Hall...and as I desire to have my name associated with it I suggest to the Senate that it be called the Winthrop Hall.[6]

The bequest also included provision for the erection or maintenance of a Church of England residential college constructed on University land.[7]

The Hackett bequest expanded the potential for immediate campus development and elevated the horizons of those involved. Large-scale integrated development became possible and the deficiencies of the Desbrowe-Annear plan, which had been under review for some time, led the Senate to explore other avenues for a revised campus plan.

REFERENCES

1. P.J. Boyce, 'The Hon. Sir J. Winthrop Hackett', unpublished paper, Battye Library.
2. ibid.
3. *Opening of Winthrop Hall, Commemoration Volume and Official Programme*, p. 9.
4. ibid.
5. F. Alexander, *Campus at Crawley*, p. 118.
6. *Opening of Winthrop Hall, Commemoration Volume and Official Programme*.
7. ibid., p. 9.

LESLIE WILKINSON

Wilkinson plan, sketch attached to Senate Minutes, November 1926 ▷

Having the opportunity to commence development of the Crawley site with a group of prominent buildings, the Senate decided to consult Leslie Wilkinson, Professor of Architecture at Sydney University from 1918, and who, as University Architect between 1919 and 1926, had been involved in the development of the Sydney campus.

Wilkinson, born in London in 1882, had held the position of Assistant Professor of Architecture at London University prior to taking up the Sydney Chair in 1918.[1] He came to Sydney University expecting that, as Professor of Architecture, he would be responsible for the University's physical development, but at that time the Government Architect was handling all building works, apparently without any recognizable planning structure.

Wilkinson pursued his expectations and, by mid-1919, had approval for him, with others, to advise on a layout of the University grounds. By the end of 1919, Wilkinson was established as University Architect, controlling all building operations. His campus plan was completed early in 1920 in time for a major building programme. Wilkinson worked in association with a number of architects practising in Sydney in order to manage the workload.[2]

Towards the completion of this programme in 1926, at the time The University of Western Australia had shown interest in enlisting his planning advice, relationships between Wilkinson and the Sydney University administration had soured and the University decided that, except for minor works, future projects were to be executed by the Government Architect. By 1928, Wilkinson was no longer University Architect but had established a large private practice outside the University, designing many houses and also a number of churches for the Church of England.[3]

Wilkinson plan, Appendix C, Hackett Memorial Buildings Competition, showing sites for buildings A, B, C, 1926 ▷

Late in 1926, Wilkinson was interviewed by the Senate of The University of Western Australia, during which discussions he presented a preliminary plan for the layout of the campus as an alternative to the Desbrowe-Annear plan. Wilkinson's proposals found favour with the Senate, which resolved

> That in accordance with Standing Order No 31 of the Senate, all decisions of Senate adopting and modifying Mr. Desbrowe-Annear's Lay-out of the University Grounds at Crawley and specifically that of 21st August 1922 allotting to the Science Departments of the blocks previously set apart for Professors' houses be rescinded.[4]

Wilkinson was subsequently appointed to assist in the preparation of competition conditions for the Hackett bequest buildings and to act as one of the assessors of the competition. His preliminary plan of 1926 specified particular sites for each of the three major building elements which were the subject of the competition. In the same year, Wilkinson was commissioned as Consulting Architect for the Physics and Chemistry, and Engineering buildings in order to oversee their design.

REFERENCES

1. D. Wilkinson, *Leslie Wilkinson. A Practical Idealist*, p. 11.
2. ibid., P. Johnson, pp. 60-68.
3. ibid., pp. 75-76.
4. *Senate Minutes*, 13 December 1926.

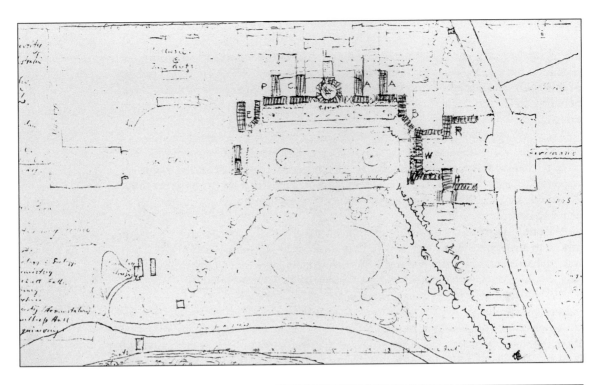

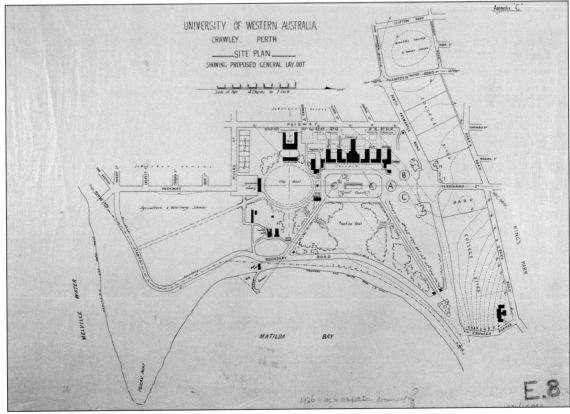

WILKINSON PLAN

The Wilkinson plan dated 1927 moved Desbrowe-Annear's main entrance from the intersection of Fairway and the Perth Fremantle Road to the Ferdinand Street axis. The entrance was strengthened by the location of a Court of Honour, now Whitfeld Court; the Great Hall; the Great Court; an object, probably a memorial, on the site now occupied by the Reid Library; an oval; a gymnasium and armoury, on the site now occupied by Chemistry; and a parade ground.

The north-east and south-east axes of the Desbrowe-Annear plan were retained but not in the same locations. Sites for residential colleges remained on the north side of the Perth Fremantle Road at the expense of provisions for houses for professors. Agriculture and Veterinary Science were returned to the southern campus. Engineering had already been committed to the area around the Shenton homestead and was shown to remain in that location. The 1927 plan showed Hackett Drive as Boundary Road and Princess Road as Mary Street.

Desbrowe-Annear's Practice Oval for Colleges, west of Hampden Road, was retained as a Women's Hockey Ground, and the site for the Conservatorium of Music remained immediately west of the main oval.

The provisions for professors' houses deleted from the 1922 Desbrowe-Annear plan and 1925 Public Works Department versions of the plan were replaced by narrow strips adjacent to Parkway and Myers Street and noted on the 1927 plan as 'Staff Houses'. A similar width strip was also shown adjacent to Fairway on the 1941 and 1952 campus plans.

Wilkinson's plan was notable for the congestion of buildings to the west of the north-south axis. Apart from Guild, Engineering, Agriculture and Veterinary Science, all buildings south of the Perth Fremantle Road were shown located on the higher Fairway flank of the campus.

It has been assumed that Desbrowe-Annear had planned for a student population of around 2,000 and Wilkinson for up to 3,000 students. When it was realized that the campus population would inevitably exceed these numbers, the constraints of the Wilkinson plan became apparent. The tight monolithic layout of the main body of buildings denied flexibility and made expansion of departments difficult.

In 1927, as part of his role as Consulting Architect, Wilkinson prepared a design for the Physics building. The two-storey design showed accommodation for Physics, with Chemistry as a future extension. No progress was made with the building because of a shortage of funds and also because there was disagreement over the site and some user conflict over the details of the proposed building. In 1928, without consulting Wilkinson, the Senate changed the site for the building to be adjacent to the north-west corner of the Great Court where Wilkinson had located Arts. This change, which was communicated to Wilkinson early in 1929, became the first of several modifications to the 1927 plan.[1]

It appears that Wilkinson did not attempt to illustrate the third dimension of his campus plan until early in 1930. Minutes of a meeting of the Senate on 17 March 1930 refer to 'A letter from Professor Wilkinson with studies of the elevation and plan for the complete group of University Buildings expressing the hope that these might be dedicated in Dr. Saw's memory'.[2] Saw had been Chancellor from 1922 until his death in 1929. The drawing, dated 1 January 1930, illustrated a detailed plan and elevation entitled 'Preliminary Study for Main Facade of Academic Group' (Science, Library and Arts).

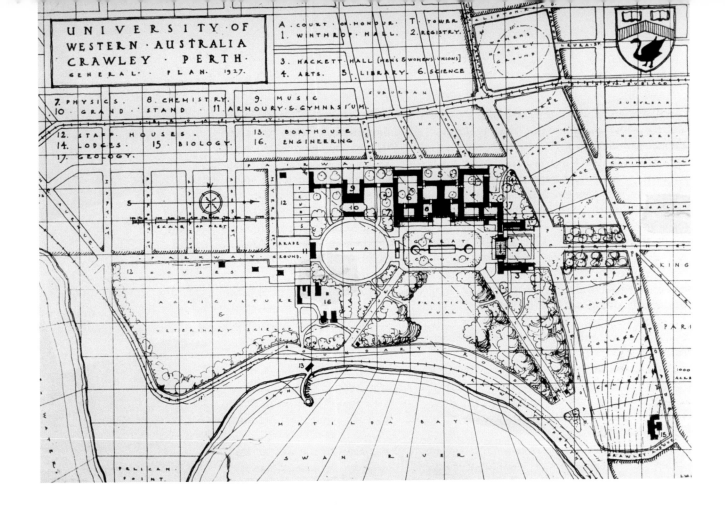

Wilkinson plan, 1927

Earlier, in 1928, architects Rodney H. Alsop and A. Bramwell Smith had prepared a rendered east elevation of this same group of buildings from Wilkinson's campus plan but with a domed Library in lieu of Wilkinson's faceted roof. In the same year, Alsop and Smith also developed their elevational presentation into an aerial perspective depicting the main elements of the campus.

Architect Marshall Clifton redrew the Alsop-Smith perspective to include additional detail such as Shenton House and Somerville Auditorium. Apparently Clifton's 'Birds Eye View' was prepared for display at ceremonies involved in the laying of the foundation stones of the Hackett Memorial Buildings in 1929.[3]

The Public Works Department prepared several versions of the east elevation of the main academic group in what became a period of open contest between Government and private architects for commissions on the campus.

R. Summerhayes and A.R. Baxter Cox, Associated Architects, presented yet another version of Wilkinson's elevation in December 1933.

REFERENCES

1. F. Alexander, *Campus at Crawley*, p. 598.
2. *Senate Minutes*, 17 March 1930.
3. F. Alexander, *Campus at Crawley*, p. 600.

RODNEY HOWARD ALSOP

Rodney Alsop was born in Kew, Victoria, in 1881 and as early as 1896 showed considerable artistic talents, at this time spending Saturday mornings in the offices of Melbourne architects Hyndman and Bates (later to become Bates, Smart and McCutcheon).

Alsop commenced his architectural career in 1901 articled to Hyndman and Bates and was admitted to the Victorian Institute of Architects in 1906 when he formed a partnership with F.L. Klingender. This partnership lasted until 1920, and between 1921 and 1924 Alsop joined the partnership Henderson, Alsop and Martin.

Alsop's practice prior to his involvement with the Hackett Memorial Buildings included a variety of houses, commercial and hospital work, churches and landscape architecture projects.

His early domestic work was influenced by English Cottage architecture but he later developed a strong Mediterranean style which is admirably expressed in his work on the Crawley campus and several houses designed for the suburbs of Perth.

Despite constant suffering from asthma, Alsop was responsible for a large volume of work and was an accomplished draftsman, which is evidenced by the vast number of sketches and details produced for the Hackett Memorial Buildings. His partnership with his contemporary Austin Bramwell Smith lasted only from 1931 until Alsop's death in 1932.

REFERENCE

The above details were supplied by David H. Alsop.

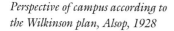

Perspective of campus according to the Wilkinson plan, Alsop, 1928

*Elevation of academic buildings
according to the Wilkinson plan,
Alsop and Bramwell Smith, 1928*

*Perspective of campus according to
the Wilkinson plan, Marshall
Clifton, 1929*

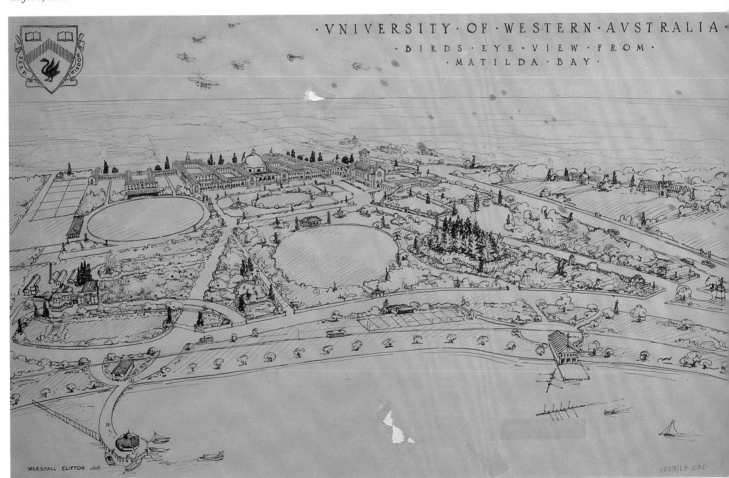

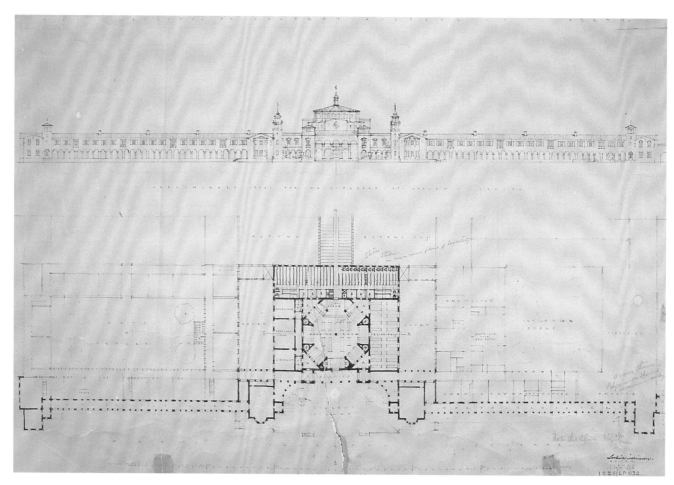

Plan and elevation of main academic buildings, Wilkinson, 1930

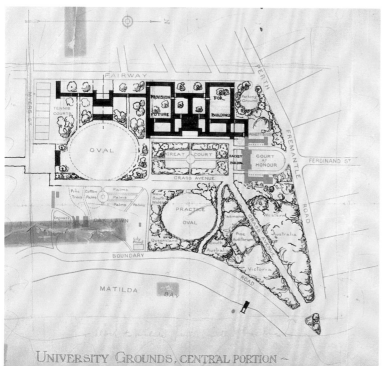

Landscape proposal for the central portion of the site, 1930, probably by G.M. Nunn, Lecturer in Surveying

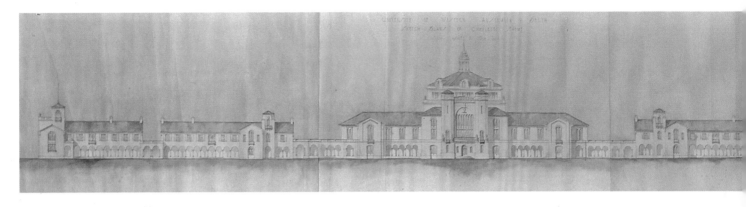

*Elevation of academic buildings
according to the Wilkinson plan,
Public Works Department, circa
1929*

*Plan and elevation of academic
buildings according to the Wilkinson plan,
Summerhayes and Baxter Cox, 1933*

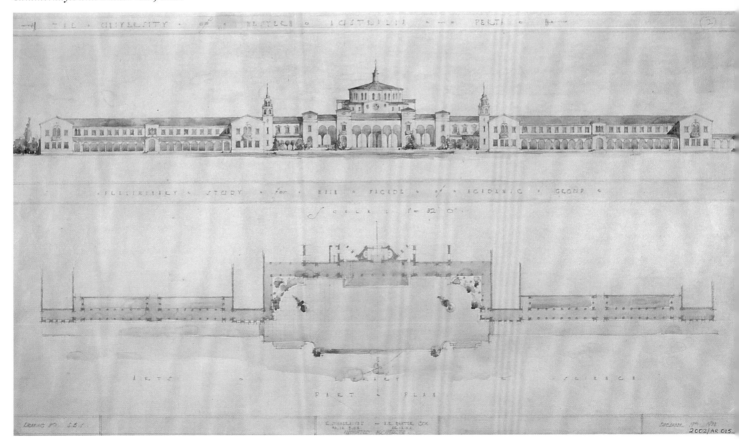

WINTHROP HALL COMPETITION

Hackett's will stipulated that the designs for 'the Winthrop Hall' should be selected after open architectural competition. At a special meeting of the Senate on 29 November 1926, it was decided to invite entries from Australasia, Britain and America. Premiums were fixed at £300 first prize, £200 second prize and £100 third prize, and the three assessors were to be an architect nominated by the Senate – Wilkinson, an architect nominated by the President of the Royal Australian Institute of Architects WA (Inc.) – A.R.L. Wright, and a nominee of the Senate – Chancellor Athelston Saw.

The competition in fact called for designs for a Great Hall, accommodation for Administration and Student facilities, and temporary accommodation for a Library and Faculty of Arts. The particular sites for the hall and two other major elements of the required accommodation were located by Professor Leslie Wilkinson on his preliminary campus plan presented to the Senate at the November 1926 meeting.[1]

The competition, which produced fifty-two entries, was judged in August 1927 and won by Melbourne architects Rodney H. Alsop and Conrad H. Sayce. The second premium was awarded to Donald H. McMorran, Harrow-on-the-Hill, England, and the third premium to Gunmer and Ford, Auckland, New Zealand. The Perth firm of architects E. Summerhayes and Son was placed fourth.

The assessors' report stated:

> In our opinion design No 141 is outstanding in its excellence…In deciding on the awards a slight difficulty has arisen owing to the fact that two designs viz Nos 141 and 137 are in all essential points the same. This similarity is so pronounced that we feel justified in considering them as one design with an alternative.[2]

Entries Nos 141 and 137 had identical plan layouts but varying elevational treatments and were bracketed together by the assessors to be awarded first prize. The assessors showed a definite preference for Entry No. 141.[3]

Sayce was in the employ of Alsop and worked on an office submission for the competition, at the same time preparing his own version of the submission away from the office. Alsop was suffering an illness in a nursing home during the preparation of the office entry and had communication with the office through his office manager, Bramwell Smith, who became Alsop's partner when Sayce left for South Africa. It was agreed between Alsop and Sayce that both versions of the design would be submitted under both names, with the intent that should either design be successful the two architects would combine forces to execute the project.[4]

Alsop and Sayce did combine to develop Sayce's design but fell out over the design of the tower of Winthrop Hall. Sayce had produced an 'original tower design' which Alsop, without Sayce's agreement, replaced with an 'Italian campanile'. Sayce suffered some discontent because it was his competition design that was being developed and Alsop was the one communicating with the University.

Born in Somerset in 1888, Sayce studied architecture in Sunderland and migrated to Australia around 1912, but did not pursue his architectural career until 1925 when he joined Alsop's office. After falling out with Alsop, he left Australia in 1931 for South Africa where he practised until his death in 1966 at the age of 78.

Alsop attended to the successful completion of the Hackett Memorial Buildings but died in Melbourne in 1932 after an illness, at the age of 51.[5]

The report accompanying Entry No. 141 could

> ...not justify our facing the buildings with stone – with Donnybrook stone, that is, for we would not entertain the thought of Cottesloe [stone] because it darkens so much with age. So we suggest a cement-faced treatment with Donnybrook stone dressings and granite columns to the lower arcades of Winthrop Hall.[6]

The report accompanying Entry No. 137 '...could not afford the architecture of Guildford Chapel' and recommended that 'The windows of the Administration building should look right over the Union block and obtain a full view of Perth across the water'. Also:

> ...not being personally conversant with the available building materials mentioned in the conditions of this competition it is difficult to definitely advise on the subject at this stage.
>
> The funds available for the accommodation required render any extensive use of grey granite impossible and it is suggested that the use of this be confined to the external columns of the lower arcade of Winthrop Hall, the columns, supporting the Hall floor, being of concrete painted in bright colours. The external columns would carry the rusticated arches of Donnybrook stone supporting the upper arcade with columns of the same material but with arches of Cottesloe stone, the upper walls of Winthrop Hall being also of Cottesloe stone with dressings of Donnybrook.[7]

Both competition entries showed the Union building (Hackett Hall) as a part two-storey, part single-storey building with a pitched roof over the northern single-storey kitchen services section, second floors over the northern dining rooms and also the southern games and men's common rooms, with a flat roof over the single-storey connecting wing. Views were obviously meant to be gained over the single-storey flat roof section.

Much of the architectural success of the Crawley campus comes from a response to the Entry No. 141 report – 'We wish the buildings to stand out against their setting and should like the prevailing colour to be a warm or light buff...'.

Competitors were required to submit cost estimates with their designs. Entry No. 141 was estimated to cost £150,000 and Entry No. 137 £157,000.[8]

Rodney Alsop, in the *Opening of Winthrop Hall Commemoration Volume and Official Programme*, April 1932, declared:

> 'Renaissance' is the only definite term that can be given as the style of the Hackett Buildings – and the Renaissance began in Italy...it was found necessary to return to the fountain head, and develop directly from the early Renaissance of the sunny climate of Italy, where mass and form count more than the applied detail, which in the greyer climate of England became such an important feature of the style.

The potpourri of details included 'dressings' of fine Donnybrook stone to relieve the coarser, cushion faced limestone walls, 'Venetian' mosaic insets and 'winged beast' friezes from Persepolis.

In a letter dated 2 September 1927 to Alsop and Sayce confirming tele-grammed advice of their first prize and enclosing a cheque for £300, Vice-Chancellor Whitfeld requested that the Administration wing of the group of buildings be documented first, then the Student building and finally Winthrop Hall, because of the University's urgent need to move from Irwin Street.[9]

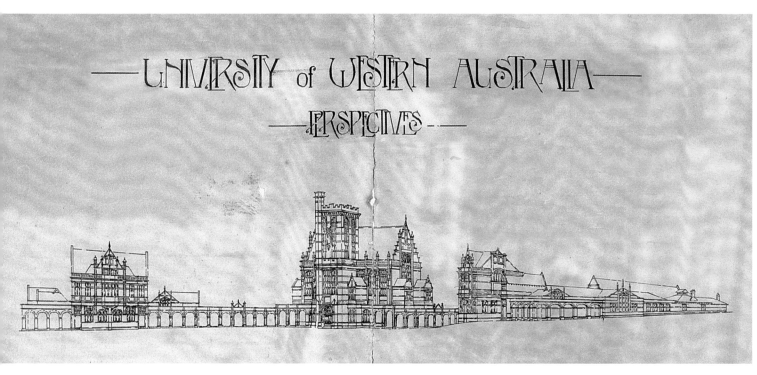

Competition Entry No. 128 by Perth
architect A.B. Rieusset, 1927. Perspective

West elevation

Site plan

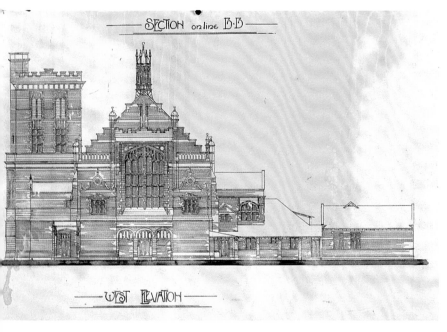

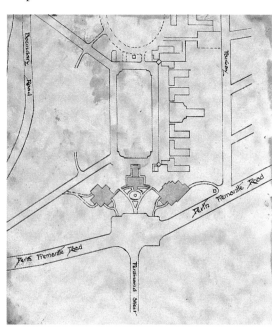

*Competition Entry No. 137 by
Rodney H. Alsop and Conrad H.
Sayce, 1927*

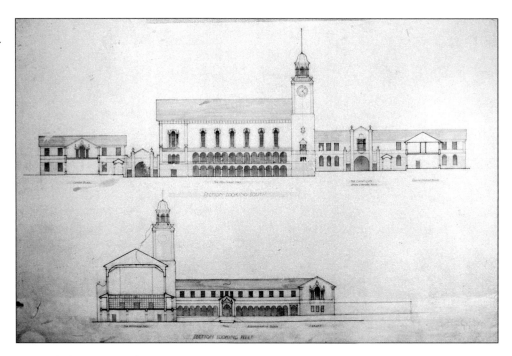

Sections looking south and west

Plan two

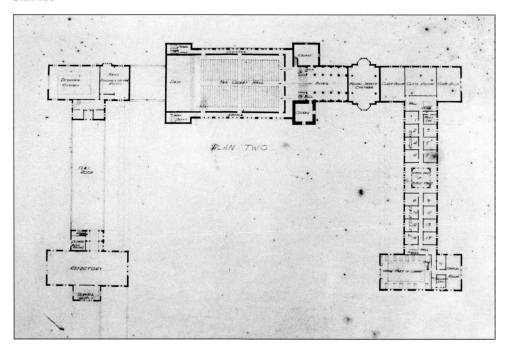

Competition Entry No. 137 by
Rodney H. Alsop and Conrad H.
Sayce, 1927

Interior perspective, Winthrop Hall

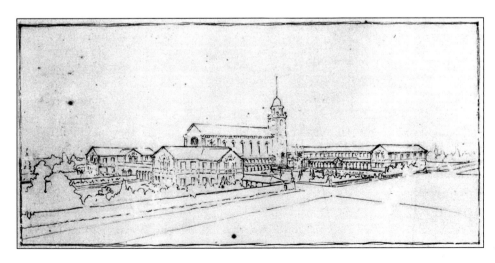

Perspective of competition buildings

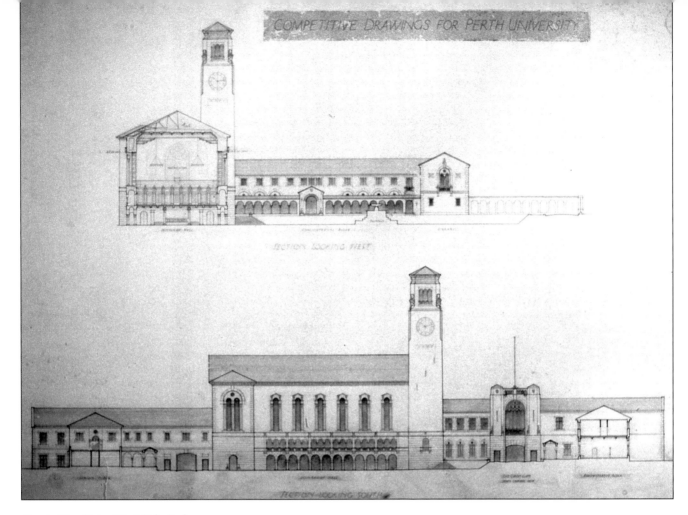

*Competition Entry No. 141 by Rodney
H. Alsop and Conrad H. Sayce, 1927*

*Section looking west, section
looking south (above),
and plan three (below)*

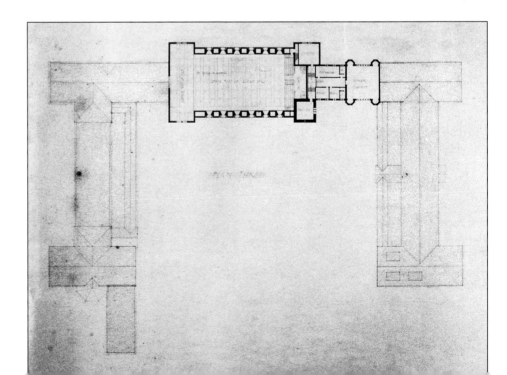

29

Competition Entry No. 141 by
Rodney H. Alsop and Conrad H.
Sayce, 1927. Half sheet of details

Competition Entry No. 141 by
Rodney H. Alsop and Conrad H.
Sayce, 1927. Half sheet of details

During the documentation stage, it became evident that building costs were likely to exceed the funds available, and in February 1928 the Senate decided 'That the design of the Students' Building [Hackett Hall] in the Architectural Competition should be reduced by the elimination for the present of the top storey'.[10]

At a Senate meeting in March 1928, 'It was decided that alternative tenders should be called for facings of the Hackett Buildings (a) with Cottesloe stone, and (b) with stucco', and, regarding the type of roof tile, that 'the Spanish tiles should be used in preference to the Marseilles tiles'. At the same meeting, the Senate agreed 'to the modification of the tower for the Winthrop Hall as suggested by Mr. Alsop. It was suggested that the installation of an electric clock should be considered.'[11]

Tender documents for the Hackett Memorial Buildings were approved by the Senate at a meeting on 18 June 1928, and models of the Administration block and Hackett (Students') Hall were received and inspected by members of the Senate at a meeting on 16 July 1928.

Eleven building companies submitted alternative tenders for stone cladding and for 'synthetic stone' and brickwork in July 1928. The company Hawkins and Son submitted the lowest tender for the stone alternative in the amount of £228,828, followed by Donald £230,725, Brine and Sons £232,868, and Allwood £234,800. Allwood submitted the lowest tender for the synthetic stone and brickwork alternative in the amount of £195,600, followed by Brine and Sons £196,638, Sedgley £196,660, and Todd Bros £198,730. The Senate decided that no tenders would be accepted and the architects were requested to negotiate costs with the lowest tenderers.[12]

Negotiations with Hawkins and Son failed, and A.T. Brine and Sons – the third lowest tenderer for the stone alternative and second lowest for the synthetic stone and brickwork alternative – revised its tender to a sum of £169,689. The Senate instructed that building costs were not to exceed £181,179.[13]

The foundation stones of Hackett Hall and Winthrop Hall were laid in separate ceremonies in April 1929 in the presence of Lady (Hackett) Moulden and Hackett's son, Mr (later, Lieutenant-General Sir) John Winthrop Hackett. The Administration building was constructed without the benefit of such a ceremony.

To meet the escalating costs of the buildings during construction, the Senate requested Alsop to recommend cost savings 'which would not impair the architecture of the buildings'. It had been intended to render the concrete structure of the Hall, and one of several savings approved by the Senate was 'The omission of plastering to undercroft and elsewhere'.[14]

Alsop recommended further:

> I am of the opinion that much of the brick interior walling and vaulting is too good to be covered. I therefore recommend that this be properly jointed and treated to finish as brickwork. This applied to portions of the Foyer, upper Foyer and passage to the Senate Chamber.[15]

While the Winthrop Hall and Administration buildings were completed as designed with limestone walling and Donnybrook stone dressings, the Student building (Hackett Hall) employed these materials in some elements only, the main single-storey structure being constructed of the more economical rendered brickwork.

Some criticism was levelled at the winning design, as evidenced by an article in a local newspaper quoting a Sydney publication:[16]

When…the winning designs were published in the press, the public generally, the architectural and building community particularly were astounded and could scarcely believe that the successful designs were the best that the architectural brains of Australia and other parts of the world could formulate…The stunted mill chimney at the end of the building…so clearly recalls the recent attempt to inflict a similar erection at the Sydney University that further comment about the adjudicator [Wilkinson] is needless…A mixture of gable on the long roof and hips over the transept is pathetic.

The article carried a drawing captioned THE PROPOSED UNPREPOSSESSING INTERIOR OF THE WINTHROP HALL with the comment '…it should be supposed that the illustration was intended for a bush court house in a C grade country town', and an alternative prepared by another competitor captioned AN ATTRACTIVE INTERIOR DESIGN with the comment 'There is a Tudor suggestion about this simple and dignified interior…which satisfies the eye and should be a success from an acoustic standpoint'.

Criticism waned as the buildings took shape and the architectural strength of the composition became apparent. It was not long before it became generally accepted that the Hackett Memorial Buildings presented one of the finest architectural statements in Australia.

The Vice-Chancellor moved to the new Administration building in March 1930 and the first lectures were given there in July of the same year. The opening of Winthrop Hall took place on 15 April 1932, with Hackett's daughter Patricia officiating at the ceremony.[17]

The Hackett Memorial Buildings were awarded the Royal Institute of British Architects triennial Bronze Medal in 1932 for excellence in design.

Despite several cost-cutting exercises during construction, the final cost of the Hackett Memorial Buildings was around £250,000.

REFERENCES

1. *Senate Minutes*, 29 November 1926.
2. Assessors' Report, August 1927, Minute Book marked Architectural Competition, The University of Western Australia.
3. ibid.
4. Papers collected by Professor Fred Alexander, University File No. 2424.
5. ibid.
6. Minute Book marked Private, Architectural Competition, The University of Western Australia.
7. ibid.
8. ibid.
9. Papers collected by Professor Fred Alexander, University File No. 2424.
10. *Senate Minutes*, 7 February 1928.
11. *Senate Minutes*, 19 March 1928.
12. *Senate Minutes*, 6 August 1928.
13. *Senate Minutes*, 28 August 1928.
14. *Senate Minutes*, 17 November 1930.
15. *Senate Minutes*, 15 December 1930.
16. *Sunday Times*, 20 November 1927, quoting 'Building', October 1927.
17. F. Alexander, *Campus at Crawley*, p. 136.

*Interior perspective of Winthrop
Hall, Alsop, 1928*

*Competition Entry No. 125 by E.
Summerhayes and Son, 1927*

*Interior perspective of Winthrop
Hall*

*Interior perspective of Senate Room,
Alsop and Sayce, 1928*

*Perspective of competition buildings
with single-storey Hackett Hall,
Alsop and Sayce, 1928*

Winthrop Hall, north elevation to Court of Honour, circa 1928,
Rodney H. Alsop, FRIBA; Conrad H. Sayce name blanked out

Administration building, elevations, circa 1928, Rodney H.
Alsop, FRIBA; Conrad H. Sayce name blanked out

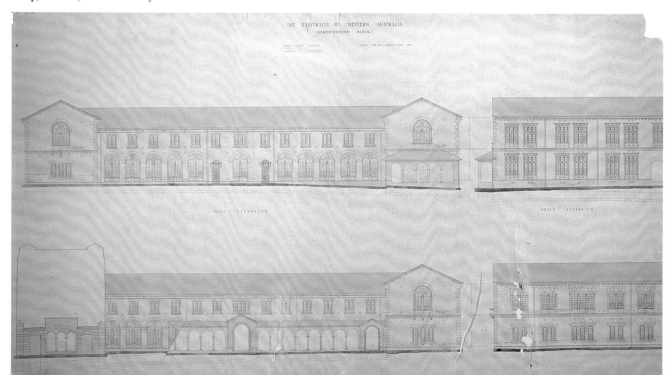

Stair detail, Hackett Hall, circa 1931

Frank Glennon (on left of lady), Alsop's resident architect for the Hackett Memorial Buildings, circa 1928

*Cartoon for mosaic above the Senate
Room windows, circa 1929*

*Early model of faïence frieze for
Winthrop Hall, 1930*

*Upper portion, Great Gateway,
Alsop, 1929*

*Photographs of balconette taken by
Alsop in Italy in 1925*

*Detail of balconette for Winthrop
Hall tower, Alsop, 1930*

*Detail of rose window for Winthrop
Hall, Alsop, 1930*

*Photograph of rose window, the
Basilica of San Francesco, Assisi,
taken by Alsop in 1925*

DEPARTMENT OF MINING AND ENGINEERING

Early in 1914, the Department of Mining and Engineering moved from Irwin Street to occupy the Shenton homestead on the Crawley site. At a meeting on 21 June 1920, the Senate resolved that 'the Department of Mining and Engineering shall be converted into the School of Engineering and Mining'.[1] P.H. Fraenkel, appointed Lecturer in Electrical Engineering in 1915, describes the isolation and inaccessibility of the Crawley site from the other departments housed at Irwin Street.

> …the students…had to walk two miles through mud from Point Lewis, or half a mile through sand from Broadway to attend lectures. Those were the nearest points of vehicular traffic, and as the trams to Broadway took about fifty minutes to make the journey from Perth, the students required the best part of an hour to reach school. It must be realised that at that time the land between Broadway and the river and right back to Rokeby Road was nothing but dense bush. Bridle paths ran through it as did the main Perth-Fremantle road in which one was liable to be bogged in the winter and covered in dust in the summer…Not until early in 1915 was the tram along the Mounts Bay Road, which till then terminated at Point Lewis, extended to a point three chains within the present University grounds and then later in the same year extended to Nedlands.
>
> The isolation of the school may well be gathered from the fact that before June 1921 no police was established at Nedlands where now two policemen are considered necessary. The absence of the guardians of the law made itself felt in the campus established on what is now known as the Parks and Gardens Board's ground. The camps in the new mining districts of today are palaces compared to the ramshackled sheds then erected along the river right in front of the school.
>
> The school itself consisted of Shenton's villa, together with a large stable, some low lean-to sheds and one milking shed…The villa was a brick and stone structure with an iron roof, consisting of a ground floor with three rooms and an upper storey with four rooms and a bathroom. From this a wing had been built of bricks manufactured from the clay deposits on the site itself. The wing had three rooms on the ground floor and three on the top floor. At the end of 1913 a verandah was built around one half of the villa and later in 1918 was enclosed…[2]

The Shenton homestead and its outbuildings could not cope with the expanding school and in 1927, concurrent with the preparation of Wilkinson's campus layout, the second permanent building was constructed for the University immediately north of the Shenton homestead to designs prepared by the Public Works Department. Although part of Wilkinson's Consulting Architect's brief, it would be surprising if he had viewed and approved the design of the two- and three-storey brick building sited in an uncomfortable relationship with the homestead.

Survey of Crawley house (Shenton homestead) and outbuildings, Public Works Department, 1911 ▷

Measured plans of Crawley house (Shenton homestead), Public Works Department, 1911 ▷

REFERENCES

1. *Senate Minutes*, 21 June 1920.
2. P.H. Fraenkel, Reminiscences from the School of Mining & Engineering of The University of Western Australia, a paper presented to the Institution of Engineers, Battye Library.

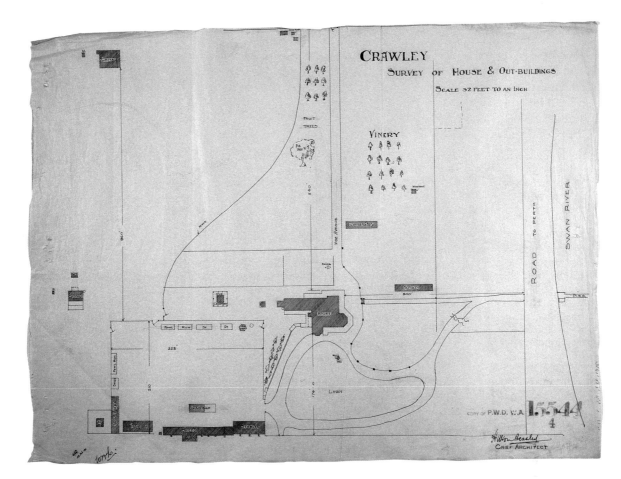

CRAWLEY

SURVEY OF HOUSE & OUT-BUILDINGS

SCALE 32 FEET TO AN INCH

VINERY

FRUIT TREES

ROAD TO PERTH

SWAN RIVER

LAWN

COPY OF P.W.D. W.A. 15544

Hilton Beasley
CHIEF ARCHITECT

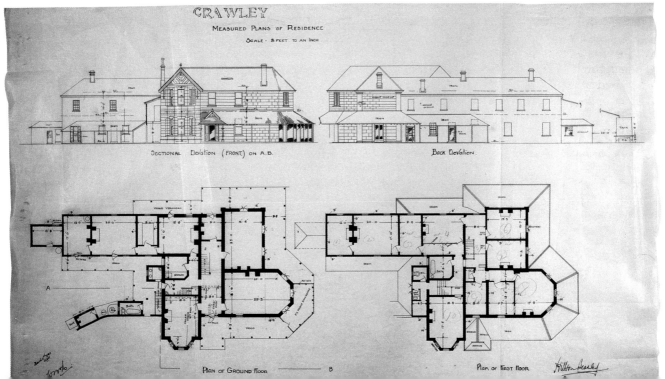

CRAWLEY

MEASURED PLANS OF RESIDENCE

SCALE · 8 FEET TO AN INCH

Sectional Elevation (Front) on A.B.

Back Elevation.

Plan of Ground Floor

Plan of First Floor

Hilton Beasley

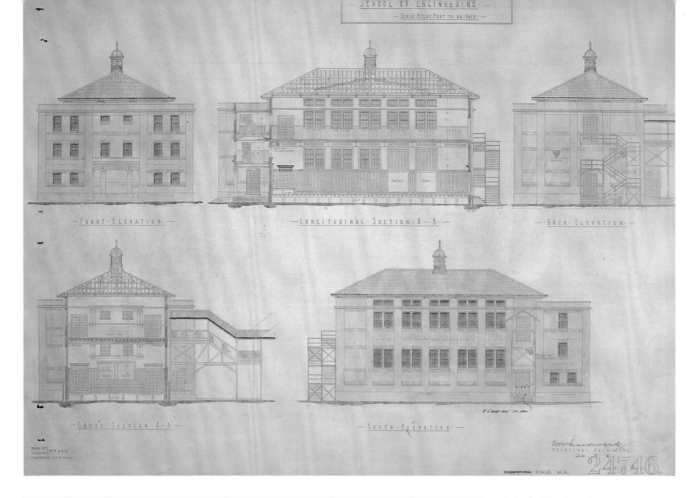

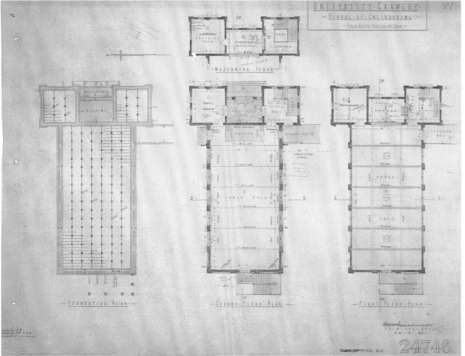

*School of Engineering,
Public Works Department, 1926*

Sections and elevations (above)

Plans

*School of Engineering, Public Works
Department, 1926*

Detail of halls

PHYSICS AND CHEMISTRY BUILDING

After Wilkinson's presentation of a design for the Physics building in 1927, there was little communication between the University and Wilkinson until mid-1929, when he was requested to comment on working drawings for the Physics and Chemistry building, dated June 1929 and prepared by the Government Architect, on the new site at the north-west corner of the Great Court. The project was aborted because of a lack of funds.[1]

The battle for commissions continued, with Rodney Alsop, supported by Vice-Chancellor Whitfeld, preparing yet another set of abortive drawings for the building in 1931. These drawings were presented to the Senate on 16 March 1931. The main facade to the Great Court was to be constructed in limestone with concrete columns. The elevation to the Perth Fremantle Road was to be clad partly in stone and partly in brickwork similar to the materials used in Hackett Hall. The sketches were approved and the Senate authorized the preparation of working documents.[2]

It is notable that Alsop submitted designs for the Robes for the Chancellor at the same meeting, and these were also approved.[3]

Despite the Senate's approval of Alsop's design for the building, there was some dissatisfaction with the design, which was described as 'unsuccessful', but with a failing economy work on the building was again postponed.

Alsop's death in 1932 terminated his involvement with the project, and late in the same year Physics and Chemistry moved to the Crawley campus to reoccupy, temporarily, the timber and iron buildings which the Public Works Department had relocated from Irwin Street. These buildings, with others, were reconstructed in the north-west corner of the Crawley site adjacent to Fairway, causing some concern to the local authority and local residents who considered the appearance of the structures to be detrimental to property values.[4] The last of these structures were not removed from the Crawley campus until August 1988.

In 1933, architects Baxter Cox and Summerhayes were commissioned to prepare the sixth of a series of plans for the Physics and Chemistry building. Designs were approved by the Senate in April 1934 and the building was opened in October 1935.[5]

The design of the building, which followed the style set by Alsop and Sayce in the Hackett Memorial Buildings and in part the materials proposed by Alsop in his 1931 design for the building, received considerable criticism, particularly because of the cost of repeating the 'Alsop-Sayce' colonnade which was done at the insistence of Vice-Chancellor Whitfeld. Norman Wilsmore, foundation Professor of Chemistry, understandably resented the loss of laboratory and teaching space to pay for this colonnade.[6]

Alfred Richard Baxter Cox was born at Cue, Western Australia, and was educated in Perth. He enlisted in the Army and served in the First World War, returning to Australia in 1920 with the rank of Lieutenant.[7] He worked for some time with his father, Alfred Edward Cox, who was born in Adelaide in 1869 and who had been a partner in the architectural firm of C.L. Oldham and A.E. Cox established in 1905.[8]

A.R. Baxter Cox temporarily abandoned his architectural practice to act as foreman to builders A.T. Brine and Sons for the erection of the Hackett Buildings, thus becoming familiar with Rodney Alsop's methods of construction. In 1933, he won an architectural competition for Anzac House, which was constructed on the original University site at Irwin Street.[9]

A.R. Baxter Cox died in 1958.

The University archives contain illustrations of a Public Works Department design of a combined Chemistry and Agriculture building, dated 1929, and an alternative design for a combined Chemistry, Agriculture and Physics building, undated, both buildings being located on the west side of the Great Court.

Illustrations exist of a 1931 Alsop and Bramwell Smith design of a combined Chemistry, Agriculture and Physics building on the same site.

Architects Baxter Cox and Leighton, with R. Summerhayes, prepared a design of a six-floor Library building, including a basement with an additional small floored tower of which the drawings depict a 'typical floor'. The drawings held in the archives are floor plans only and are dated 29 May 1939.

The various architects apparently associated in various combinations, with one architect's name appearing first on some designs and second on others.

REFERENCES

1. F. Alexander, *Campus at Crawley*, p. 598.
2. *Senate Minutes*, 16 March 1931.
3. ibid.
4. F. Alexander, *Campus at Crawley*, p. 141.
5. ibid., p. 142.
6. ibid.
7. *Australia's Fighting Sons of the Empire*, 1920, p. 1.
8. J.S. Battye, *The Cyclopedia of Western Australia*, vol. 1, p. 628.
9. *West Australian*, 29 November 1933.

Physics and Chemistry building,
Public Works Department, 1929

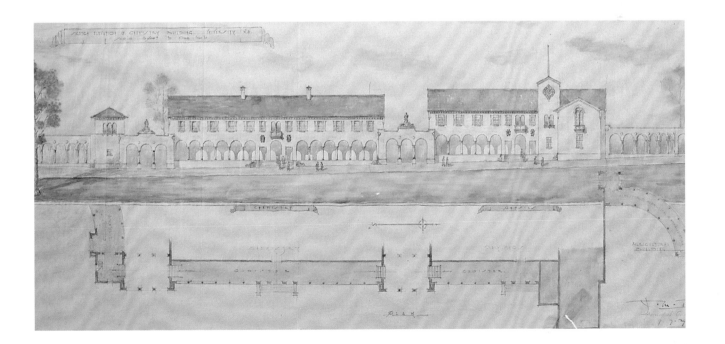

47

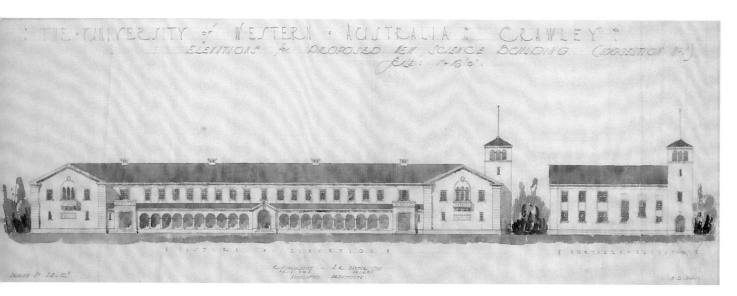

Physics and Chemistry building,
Suggestion No. 1, Baxter Cox and
Summerhayes, 1934

Physics and Chemistry building,
sketch approved by the Buildings
Committee, Baxter Cox and
Summerhayes, 1934

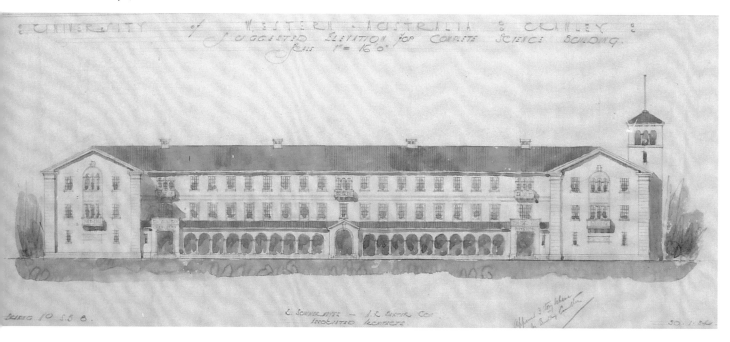

Tuart House

The first official residence for the University's Vice-Chancellor was designed by Baxter Cox and Summerhayes in 1934 and constructed adjacent to St George's College and the Biology and Geology building. Named Tuart House after the Tuart trees on the site at the time of construction, the two-storey neo-Georgian brick building apparently suited Vice-Chancellors Whitfeld and Currie but not Prescott who, as Vice-Chancellor from 1953, preferred a residence off the campus. Early in 1960, Prescott vacated the house, and the building was converted for use by the Department of Music.[1]

Music moved to the first stage of its new building adjacent to Somerville Auditorium in 1976. Tuart House currently provides facilities for the Festival of Perth and University of Western Australia Press.

Reginald Summerhayes graduated as Bachelor of Science in Engineering at The University of Western Australia in 1921 after war service in France with the Royal Engineers between 1916 and 1919. After working with architects in Singapore between 1921 and 1925, he joined his father, Edwin Summerhayes, who had commenced practice in Perth in 1897. Reginald Summerhayes was in continuous practice as an architect until his death in 1965, except for a period from 1939 to 1946 when he served in the Australian Imperial Force with the rank of Lieutenant-Colonel.[2] The firm E. Summerhayes and Son was placed fourth in the Winthrop Hall competition in 1927.[3] The practice became Summerhayes and Associates in 1952.

REFERENCES

1. F. Alexander, *Campus at Crawley*, p. 720.
2. R.J. Dyer, 'Contributors', *The Architect*, vol. 8, no. 18, 1965.
3. Assessors' Report, August 1927, Minute Book marked Architectural Competition, The University of Western Australia.

Tuart House, 1937

INSTITUTE OF AGRICULTURE BUILDING

Wilkinson's plan for the southern campus showed the site allocated to Agriculture and Veterinary Science but with no specific building or plot locations.

The first permanent building in the southern campus was designed by architects Baxter Cox and Leighton for the Institute of Agriculture and opened in October 1938.[1] The two-storey brick building displayed Art-Deco detailing which Leighton developed in many of his other buildings.

William Thomas Leighton was born in Fremantle in 1905 and commenced his architectural career in the Fremantle offices of Allen and Nicolas.[2] Later, when working in the Perth offices of Eales and Cohen, Leighton and William G. Bennett submitted an entry in the Winthrop Hall competition which was 'Commended'.[3]

Working with Bohringer, Taylor and Johnson on the construction of the Ambassadors Theatre, Leighton began a specialized career in cinema design. He worked in Melbourne, Auckland and Sydney before returning to Perth in 1936 where, in partnership with Baxter Cox, he designed several Art-Deco buildings. The partnership was dissolved at the onset of the Second World War, after which Leighton joined the Public Works Department for a short period before being offered a partnership with the firm Hobbs, Winning and Leighton. William Leighton died in 1990.[4]

The Institute of Agriculture building was located in a 25 acre (10.12 hectare) site intended for experimental plots and glasshouses and was accessed from a cross-campus road which was opened in 1938 and which joined Myers Street to Hackett Drive.

This cross-campus link was closed in 1972, but the road surface remained and was used for internal campus access until the development of what became Prescott Court.

The Agriculture building was extended in 1956 by the Public Works Department and in 1961 by architects Duncan, Stephen and Mercer.[5]

REFERENCES

1. *Western Mail*, 19 January 1939, p. 30.
2. V. Geneve, 'William Thomas Leighton', *The Architect*, vol. 90, no. 2, 1990, p. 7.
3. Assessors' Report, August 1927, Minute Book marked Architectural Competition, The University of Western Australia.
4. V. Geneve, 'William Thomas Leighton', *The Architect*, vol. 90, no. 2, 1990, p. 7.
5. F. Alexander, *Campus at Crawley*, p. 623.

STAFF HOUSES

To provide housing for newly appointed professors and lecturers, the University commenced a programme in 1938 to construct cottages along the strips adjacent to Parkway and Myers Street and also in Monash Avenue and Arras Street, in some instances employing the University's in-house tradesmen. Funding was limited and the designs of the cottages were restricted to meet the requirements of the Workers' Homes Board.[1] The cottages were not of campus standard and at best the design and accommodation provided may be described as austere and minimal. At this date (1993), a few of the original houses, refurbished for academic use, still exist.

As Stephenson predicted in his presentation of the 1954-55 plan, many of these houses were demolished to provide sites for academic buildings such as the Sanders building, 1978; the Department of Human Movement and Recreational Studies, 1981 and 1984; a Child Care Centre, 1987; the Third General Purpose building, 1989; car parking; the Biological Sciences Library building, 1991; and a combined structure for car parking, campus workshops and general academic facilities of which the Graduate School of Management became the first tenant, 1993.

Institute of Agriculture building, original before extensions, Baxter Cox and Leighton, 1938

REFERENCE

1. F. Alexander, *Campus at Crawley*, p. 642.

51

LANDSCAPE

The Crawley campus was established in native bush and swamp lands with the location of the Department of Mining and Engineering in the Shenton homestead in 1914. Remnants of the original planting around the homestead remain and part of the avenue of Cork Oaks forms the basis of the court named Oak Lawn. The 1915 Desbrowe-Annear plan located what was to become James Oval and a north-east axis which set the orientation of Somerville Auditorium. Immediately prior to securing planning advice from Leslie Wilkinson in 1926, the University arranged with the Perth Parks and Gardens Board for its foreman gardener, Henry Campbell, to commence a planting programme on the campus south of the Perth Fremantle Road.

Wilkinson's 1927 plan located what are now Whitfeld Court, the Great Court and Riley Oval, and Campbell commenced laying out James Oval and then Riley Oval and the north-east axis, (later named) Battye Avenue, with palms radiating from Winthrop Hall. Blocks of exotic plantings were located in a formal geometric pattern around the newly constructed Hackett Memorial Buildings. After Campbell's death in 1930, the University appointed Oliver Dowell, who had worked with Campbell on the campus, as foreman gardener. Dowell had a flair for the informal and was responsible for the 'Jungle' at the northern end of the Great Court and also for softening Campbell's rigid and formal planting. He readily mixed exotic and native shrubs and trees.[1]

William (later Dr) Somerville, a member of the Senate from its establishment in 1912 to his death in 1954, took a personal and particular interest in the landscaping of the campus and, in 1927, when Wilkinson was formulating his campus plan, made proposals for 'a cathedral of trees' which could be used as an open-air auditorium while at the same time being an integral part of the campus soft landscaping.

The auditorium, which was approved by the Grounds Committee on 4 July 1927, was located adjacent and parallel to Wilkinson's north-east 'Alley' (Battye Avenue) and took the plan form of a Gothic cathedral with seating capacity for 2,500 people. The outer 'walls' comprised a 12 feet (3.66 metres) wide thicket of WA Peppermint and the 'columns', Norfolk Island Pines, the upper limbs of which formed the arched roof. All planting had been completed in 1927 and the auditorium was first used for a major event to accommodate an audience of 2,000 people at a 1945 Summer School music recital.[2] In the same year, the auditorium was named Somerville Auditorium after its originator.

According to G.G. Smith, Lecturer in Botany, the formal landscaping of Whitfeld Court with the row of Pencil Pines and two *Ficus benjamina* was the work of Rodney Alsop.[3] The two figs are actually *Ficus hillii*.

What has become known as the 'Sunken Garden' in the north-west corner of the campus is at the highest part of the campus south of Stirling Highway and was the pit from which considerable quantities of sand were excavated for use in the construction of the Hackett Memorial Buildings. The pit at that time was roughly three times the diameter of the present Sunken Garden, and observations had been made on its suitability for the construction of an amphitheatre. In 1946, sand excavated from the site of the Administration building extensions was deposited in the pit, bringing it to its present size.

In 1936, a memorial was erected to Professor E.O.G. Shann, foundation Professor of Economics, in the Sunken Garden, and Dowell, then foreman gardener, constructed a wall and base for the memorial. Dowell continued development in the garden, including construction of the two ponds and arched bridge, using waste materials from the Hackett Memorial Buildings, until his retirement in 1945.[4]

George Munns, who had worked with Dowell on the campus as assistant foreman gardener and inherited Dowell's position as foreman gardener, continued work on the Sunken Garden and was appointed Curator of Gardens in 1955. George Munns retired in 1972 after forty years' service to the University with the honorary degree of Master of Arts.

Munns developed the University grounds in accordance with the 1955 and 1962 campus plans prepared by the Consultant Architect, Professor Gordon Stephenson, assisted by John Davey who was appointed foreman gardener in 1955.

On Munns' retirement in 1972, the University created the position of University Landscape Architect and appointed Jean Verschuer on a part-time basis until 1974, when her appointment became full-time. She worked with the University Architect, Arthur Bunbury, who had been appointed to that position in 1966. In 1979, Andrew Gwynne was appointed acting foreman gardener. Jean Verschuer resigned in March 1980 but continued on a part-time basis until July of that year.

Later in 1980, Tony Morgan took up the position as University Landscape Architect working with Arthur Bunbury until Bunbury's retirement in 1985. Morgan resigned in 1987 and the full-time position of Landscape Architect lapsed, being replaced early in 1988 by an outside Consultant Landscape Architect position filled by Bill James.

The only major formal green space in the southern campus was created north of the Institute of Agriculture building with the removal of vehicular traffic from the cross-campus Myers Street reserve. This space was landscaped in 1983 and named Prescott Court after the University's third permanent Vice-Chancellor, Sir Stanley Prescott.[5]

The spaces Whitfeld Court, the Great Court, James Oval, Sunken Garden, Somerville Auditorium, Oak Lawn and Prescott Court have been protected from building development by Senate resolutions that they be maintained as 'Permanent Green Reserves'.

In 1980, Glenn Sproule was appointed acting foreman gardener following Gwynne's resignation and in 1983 accepted the appointment of Foreman (Grounds).

The position of Curator of Grounds was re-established in 1988 and filled by Glenn Sproule.[6]

In 1983, the University Architect's office was replaced by the Office of Property Services.

The Crawley campus is an integral part of a continuous landscape system comprising Kings Park, the campus and the Swan River foreshores including Point Currie. When viewed as part of this system, the tree canopy is the dominant element on the campus, penetrated only in a few places by towers and buildings. A contribution to the strength of the system is that, in general, local species were planted on the perimeter of the campus and exotic species kept to the interior spaces.

The hierarchy and disposition of the major open spaces established in the Wilkinson plan have set the pattern for the progressive development of the landscape system. The formality of the symmetrical and grand landscaping of

Whitfeld Court respects its function as the prime approach to the University. The Great Court, being the centrepiece of the northern campus and well used for informal activities, is more loosely moulded with planting but still has a scale compatible with its size and importance. The playing fields of James and Riley Ovals, each comparable in size to the Great Court, give the campus an opportunity to breathe and offer an open contrast to the increasing density of building development.

On 21 October 1980, 'The Gardens of The University of Western Australia' were entered on the Register of the National Estate as a 'Registered Place' by the Australian Heritage Commission.

On 5 June 1986, 'The Campus of The University of Western Australia' received the 'Western Australian Civic Design Award 1986' for excellence in civic design.

REFERENCES

1. G.G. Smith, 'The University Garden', *University Gazette*, 1960, p. 28.
2. W. Somerville, 'Somerville Auditorium and its Stage and the Sunken Gardens', unpublished paper, pp. 1-2.
3. G.G. Smith, 'The University Garden', *University Gazette*, 1960, p. 29.
4. ibid.
5. R.J. Ferguson & Associates, *Campus Planning Review 1990*, p. 27.
6. Bill James, *Landscape Review*, 1992, The University of Western Australia, pp. 11-12.

Aerial photograph of Crawley campus, circa 1935 ▷

Aerial photograph of Hackett Memorial Buildings with Irwin Street buildings, circa 1935

RESIDENTIAL COLLEGES

Discussions regarding residential colleges had begun as early as 1914 with the competition for the layout of the University, and in 1923 Convocation appointed a committee to investigate and report on the establishment of such colleges.[1] In this same year, St John's University Hostel made application to the Senate for land on the Crawley campus for the construction of a college.[2] In 1925, similar applications were made by the Roman Catholic, Presbyterian, Methodist and Congregational Churches and also by the Young Women's Christian Association.[3]

REFERENCES

1. *Convocation Minutes*, 28 September 1923.
2. *Senate Minutes*, 10 December 1923.
3. F. Alexander, *Campus at Crawley*, p. 513.

ST GEORGE'S COLLEGE

The University Colleges Act of 1926 provided for the allocation of lots of up to 5 acres (2 hectares) in area to each applicant, and in that year, when the details of the Hackett bequest became known, the Church of England established the Council of St George's College for the purpose of developing the first residential college on campus.[1]

In 1927, the Council commissioned Hobbs, Smith and Forbes, a firm of architects of which Lieutenant-General Sir Talbot Hobbs, a trustee of the Anglican archdiocese from 1920 to 1926, was senior partner.

Archbishop Riley, as Chairman of the Council, sought a distinctive design for the college which followed the traditional styling of Oxford and Cambridge, in direct contrast to the 'Mediterranean' styling of the Hackett Memorial Buildings and the neo-Georgian style of its immediate neighbour, the Biology and Geology building.

Plans for the college were approved in 1927, and the foundation stone of this ivy clad, red brick, Tudor styled building was laid in May 1929. The building was completed in 1930 and officially opened in April 1931.

Because of the great demand for college accommodation at the University, a fund-raising appeal was launched in 1959 to contribute to additional residential facilities. The kitchen was rebuilt and a new 'south' residential wing and Sub-Warden's house were opened in 1962 to provide accommodation for a total of 150 students. An additional 'north' residential wing was completed in 1968, both additions by architects Hobbs Winning Leighton.

REFERENCE

1. F. Alexander, *Campus at Crawley*, p. 513.

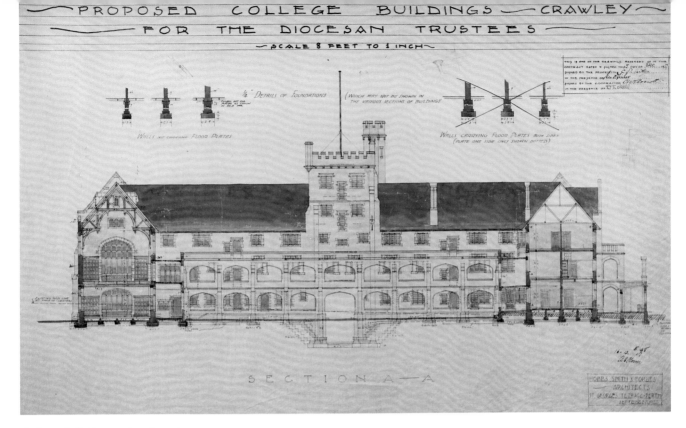

St George's College, section through
main building, 1927

St George's College, chapel, 1927

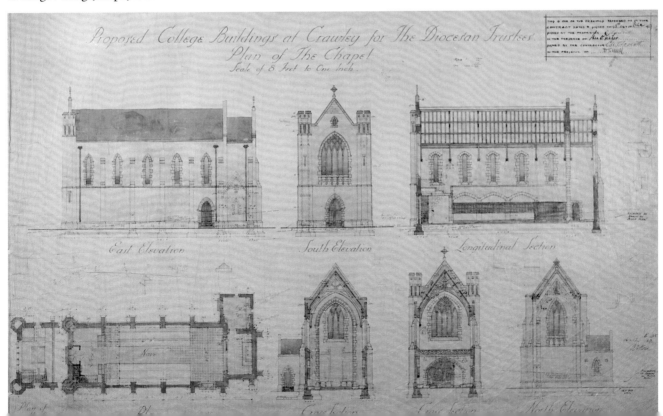

WOMEN'S COLLEGE – ST CATHERINE'S COLLEGE

In 1923, Dr Roberta Jull, a University Senator, was appointed President of the West Australian Women Graduates' Association, subsequently renamed the West Australian Association of University Women and eventually the Australian Federation of University Women (WA) Inc.[1]

In the same year, Dr Jull drew attention to the need for a residential college for women university students and, as President of the Women's College Fund Committee formed in 1928, continued to promote the need for a women's college or hostel until her resignation in 1945.[2]

The development of a women's college became a long drawn out saga with several false starts.

In 1925, the Senate resolved to reserve the 9½ acre (3.85 hectare) block on the north-western corner of the Perth Fremantle and Hampden Road intersection for the erection of 'Affiliated Colleges for Women and for the purpose of Play Grounds for the general body of women students'.[3]

This did not eventuate, and in 1960 the site was set aside for a teachers training college.

Rodney Alsop and Bramwell Smith prepared sketch plans of a 'Proposed Hostel at Crawley' (women's college) on a site to the north of the Perth Fremantle Road. The drawings only illustrate ground and first floor plans of the two-storey building and are dated November 1928.

In 1933, the Guild of Undergraduates made approaches to the Senate supporting the need for increased residential accommodation for both women and men. In December of the same year, the Senate resolved that a Women's Residential Hall be constructed on a 4 acre 1½ rood (1.77 hectare) site on the north-west corner of the Perth Fremantle Road and Winthrop Avenue intersection.[4] The hall was to be constructed with the assistance of a Government grant on a site now occupied by St Catherine's College, and the Principal Architect, A.E. Clare of the Public Works Department, prepared sketch documents and estimates of costs which exceeded the funds available. The Government agreed to an increase in its grant and the Public Works Department completed working documents of an imposing design in 1934. In October of the same year, the Government withdrew its grant because an agreement to use 70 per cent of labour from the unemployed workforce on the construction site of the Science building had not been met.[5] The Women's Residential Hall project was abandoned.

Further attempts to achieve residential accommodation for both men and women were thwarted by the outbreak of war in Europe and also by the death in July 1939 of Vice-Chancellor Whitfeld who had for many years championed the cause.

When hostilities expanded to the near regions of Australia, the United States Navy established a seaplane base on the river in 1943 adjacent to the campus. As well as base facilities on the southern campus, the Allied Works Council constructed Bachelor Officer Quarters for the Navy on the site now occupied by Currie Hall on the north-eastern corner of the intersection of Winthrop Avenue and Mounts Bay Road.

After the war, these timber-framed structures became available to the University and were converted to provide temporary residential accommodation for both men and women. What became known as 'the Hostel' opened in March 1946 with 130 students, including thirty-four women residents.[6]

The facilities provided by the Hostel were minimal, if not primitive, and pressure continued for a permanent college for women. In confirming its allocation of a 5 acre (2 hectare) site on the north-west corner of the intersection of Winthrop Avenue and Stirling Highway in 1950, the Senate found that a portion of the 16 acres (6.48 hectares) designated by Wilkinson to accommodate three colleges and some houses belonged in fact to Kings Park and not to the University. In 1955, the University's Consultant Architect, Professor Gordon Stephenson, recommended that because of the shortage of land for colleges, the site west of Winthrop Avenue be subdivided to accommodate four colleges instead of the planned three.[7]

In 1956, the Town Planning Commission reported to the University that a road widening of Stirling Highway on the north side would further reduce the area available for colleges. The Senate, in September 1956, eventually decided to subdivide the site to accommodate three colleges and finally allocated a 4½ acre (1.8 hectare) site for what was to become St Catherine's College. The first section of the college opened in June 1960 constructed to plans prepared by the Principal Architect, Public Works Department. The building was extended in 1962, 1966 and again in 1969, the last extension by architects Hobbs Winning Leighton.[8]

REFERENCES

1. N. Stewart, *St Catherine's College. From Dream to Reality*, p. 1.
2. ibid., p. 12.
3. *Senate Minutes*, 19 October 1925.
4. *Senate Minutes*, 18 December 1933.
5. F. Alexander, *Campus at Crawley*, p. 528.
6. ibid., p. 536.
7. ibid., p. 539.
8. N. Stewart, *St Catherine's College. From Dream to Reality*, p. 56.

Hostel, converted Bachelor Officer Quarters

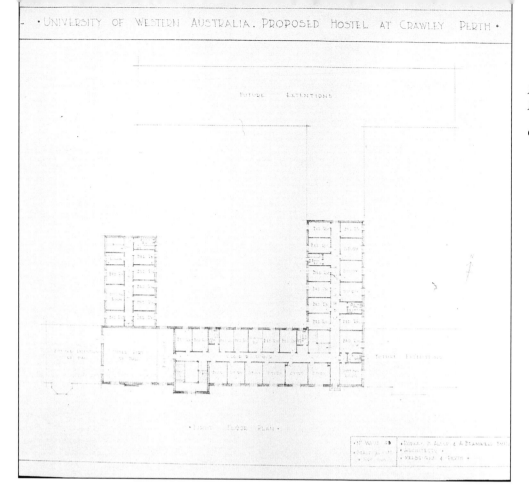

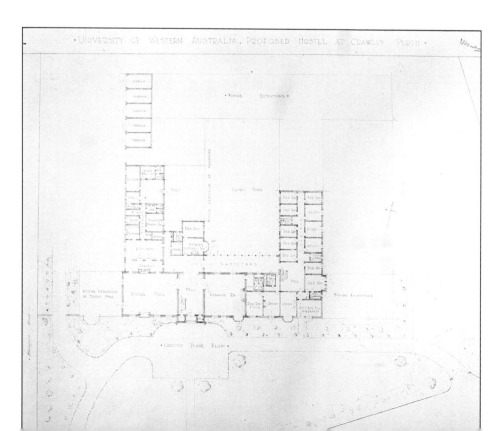

Hostel at Crawley, Alsop and Bramwell Smith, 1928

Ground floor plan

Hostel at Crawley, first floor plan

New women's hall, Public Works Department, 1934 ▷

North and south elevations (above), and ground floor plan (below)

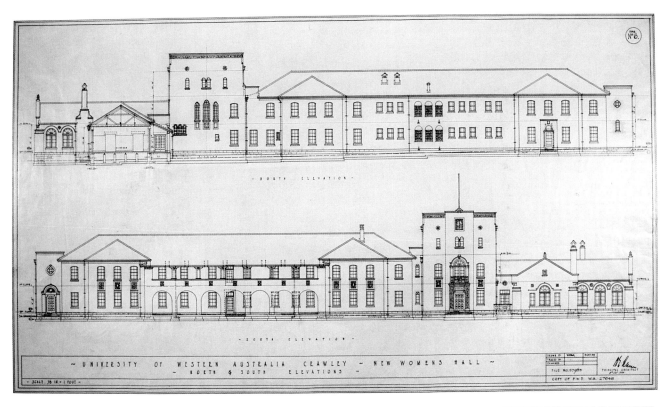

- NORTH ELEVATION -

- SOUTH ELEVATION -

- UNIVERSITY OF WESTERN AUSTRALIA CRAWLEY - NEW WOMENS HALL -
- NORTH & SOUTH ELEVATIONS -

- SCALE 16 IN. 1 FOOT -

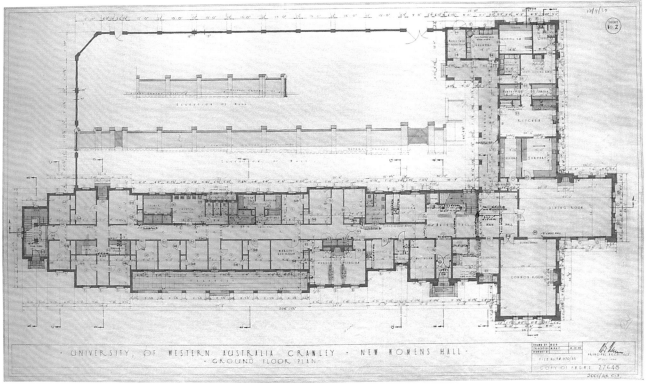

UNIVERSITY OF WESTERN AUSTRALIA CRAWLEY - NEW WOMENS HALL -
- GROUND FLOOR PLAN -

ST THOMAS MORE COLLEGE

In 1925, Archbishop Clune had made a general application to the University for allocation of a site for the construction of a Catholic residential college. After a formal application for a site was made in 1933 in accordance with the University Colleges Act 1926, the Senate approved a 5 acre (2 hectare) site on the west side of St George's College. Building construction was delayed because of lack of funds, and the application for a site had to be renewed in 1944. Until 1952, all negotiations referred to 'Newman College', but because of a possible confusion with Newman College at the University of Melbourne, the name was changed to St Thomas More College in September 1953.[1]

The first section of the college was opened in 1955, built to designs by architect Edgar Le B. Henderson.

REFERENCE

1. F. Alexander, *Campus at Crawley*, p. 550.

KINGSWOOD COLLEGE

The Rev. S.B. Fellows, President of the Methodist Conference in 1913, urged immediate affiliation of the Methodist Theological College and the newly established University, proposing that the required funds be obtained from a patron.[1] This did not eventuate, and after the 1925 general application for a college site from the Methodist Church, formal application was not made until 1955. The Church's wish that the college be both a theological and a university college proved to be not readily acceptable to the Senate, but agreement was reached in 1960 and construction of the first stage commenced in 1962 on a site on the north-eastern corner of the intersection of Hampden Road and Stirling Highway.[2]

The first-stage college was designed by architects Forbes and Fitzhardinge and opened in 1963 to seventy-six students.

REFERENCES

1. F. Alexander, *Campus at Crawley*, p. 506.
2. ibid., pp. 554-558.

CURRIE HALL

The site originally occupied by the United States Navy Bachelor Officer Quarters until being converted to a male and female student 'Hostel' in 1946 was allocated to Currie Hall in 1960.[1]

Currie Hall, the first non-collegiate residential institution on the campus, was named after Professor Sir George Currie, Vice-Chancellor of the University from 1940 to 1952, when he left for New Zealand. Women residents of the Hostel vacated the northern block of the Navy buildings to occupy St Catherine's College in 1960.[2]

The first-stage new building on the site was opened in 1967, and a second stage in 1974 was built to designs by architects Cameron Chisholm & Nicol in association with Professor Gordon Stephenson.

REFERENCES

1. F. Alexander, *Campus at Crawley*, p. 525.
2. ibid., p. 562.

ST COLUMBA COLLEGE

In 1961, the Rt Rev. A.J. Watt, Moderator of the Presbyterian Church in Western Australia, proposed to the General Assembly of that Church that action should be taken to establish a residential college on the University campus.

The General Assembly agreed to submit an application for land for the purposes of erecting a residential men's college, and the University Senate resolved in 1962 to make a 5 acre (2 hectare) site between St Catherine's and Kingswood Colleges available for the new college.

A Provisional Council was formed in 1962 to undertake preliminary planning and was authorized to examine the possibility of inviting the Congregational Church to become co-sponsors of the project. Representatives of the Congregational Church were added to the Provisional Council later in 1962.

St Columba College, named after an adventurous Irish scholar-priest who brought Christianity to Scotland, was a joint foundation of the Congregational and Presbyterian Churches, both of which now belong to the Uniting Church in Australia, Synod of Western Australia.

In 1965, the firm Howlett & Bailey was commissioned as architect for the project and construction commenced in 1970. The first-stage building was opened in 1971 to accommodate 123 students. In 1969, the College Council resolved that thirty-nine of the places planned for the first stage be reserved for women students.[1]

REFERENCE

1. D. Robinson, *Dove Rising. A Brief History of St Columba College*, pp. 1-8.

Second World War

The outbreak of war in Europe in 1939 brought the physical development of the campus to a virtual standstill until Japan entered the war in 1941 and hostilities spread to the Pacific region.

As a result of the Japanese invasion of South-East Asia and the fall of Singapore in 1942, the United States Navy in 1943 established a seaplane base on the Swan River in Matilda Bay, adjacent to the Crawley campus.

The Allied Works Council erected timber-framed buildings for the Navy on and adjacent to the campus to service Fleet Air Wing 10, which was to provide cover for allied shipping in the Indian Ocean. The Navy also occupied some University buildings in the southern campus, utilizing facilities in the Institute of Agriculture building for laboratory and photographic purposes, and Engineering Hall as a dormitory and dining room. Ovals were employed for recreational activities and as parade grounds. The University boatshed became Command Head Quarters, while the main Catalina base was located on Pelican Point. The United States Navy closed the base and vacated the buildings in 1945.

Later in 1943, Qantas Empire Airways established a second Catalina base south of Pelican Point to provide direct communication between Australia and Britain via Sri Lanka (then Ceylon). The Qantas Catalinas flew unarmed and carried mainly documents, mail, service personnel and civilian VIPs. The Qantas service was terminated in 1945.[1]

Several of the lightweight structures erected for the United States Navy on campus were retained and utilized by the University after the war, one remaining to this date (1993).

Bachelor Officer Quarters erected on the north-east corner of the intersection of Winthrop Avenue and Mounts Bay Road were converted for use as male and female residential accommodation in 1946.

These structures, known as 'the Hostel', were progressively demolished to make way for the first stage of Currie Hall in 1965 and the third stage in 1975.

Enlisted Men's Barracks erected adjacent to the east end of the Institute of Agriculture building were taken over from the United States Navy by the Royal Netherlands Navy and used as barracks for officers of its submarine fleet. The Dutch Navy vacated these barracks in 1947 and the structures were converted in 1955 and 1956 for use as temporary accommodation for the Schools of Anatomy and Physiology. A 'capping' extension was constructed in 1957 to provide facilities for Pharmacology, and the building eventually housed the Biological Sciences Library until a new Library building was constructed in 1991. The old barracks structures are currently (1993) utilized by the Departments of Agriculture and Geology.

A structure erected at the western end of the Institute of Agriculture building for use by the United States Navy as a sick bay was used by the Royal Netherlands Navy as a 'Dutch Officers' Club' until 1947; then converted to a lecture room and laboratory for the Department of Agriculture; and finally demolished to make way for the new Biological Sciences Library building in 1989.

Late in 1943, a mess hall was added to the north side of Engineering Hall and, after being vacated by the Navy, was used by the School of Engineering as a Library, Reading Room and Structures Laboratory.

In 1946, the Department of Public Works refurbished some Navy structures and erected new timber-framed buildings to the west of Shenton House for use by the

School of Engineering. In 1960, architect Marshall Clifton prepared documents for the conversion of Shenton House and Engineering Hall for use by the Faculty of Education. The 1946 School of Engineering 'Arab village' was progressively demolished around 1964.[2]

After the war, Commonwealth grants made some minor building extensions possible, and in late 1945, extensions to the Biology Department had already been completed. By 1947, the University was structuring itself for accelerating expansion to meet the demands of increasing student numbers. Funding was sought for new buildings for the School of Engineering and the main Library and also for accommodation for the Schools of Anatomy and Physiology which were required to support a new Medical School.[3]

REFERENCES

1. A.E. Williams, *From Campsite to City*, p. 173.
2. University File No. 3696, Grounds and Buildings, Use by Armed Forces, Registrar's Office, First Series.
3. F. Alexander, *Campus at Crawley*, p. 220.

Bachelor Officer Quarters, copied from United States Navy plan

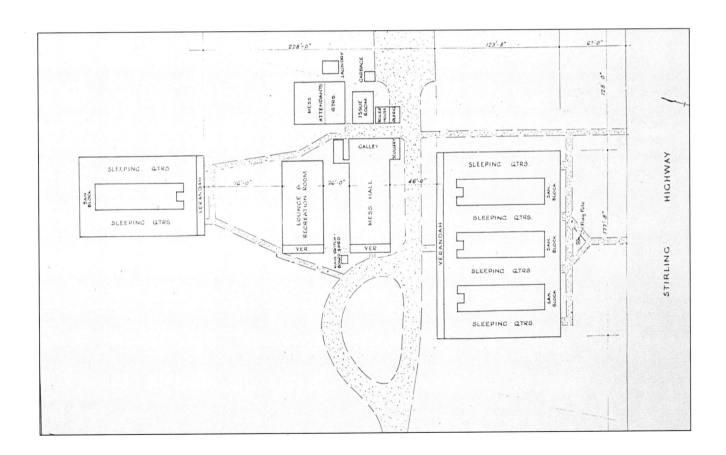

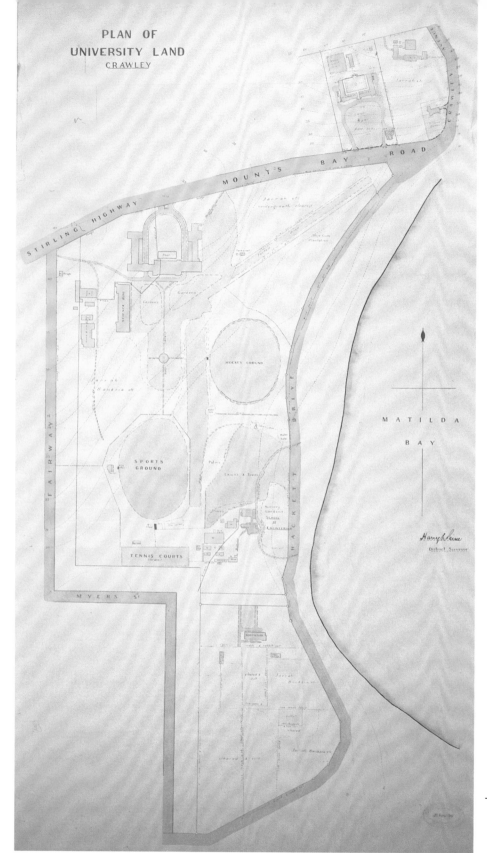

PLAN OF
UNIVERSITY LAND
CRAWLEY

*Campus layout, District Surveyor,
Harry Paine, 1941*

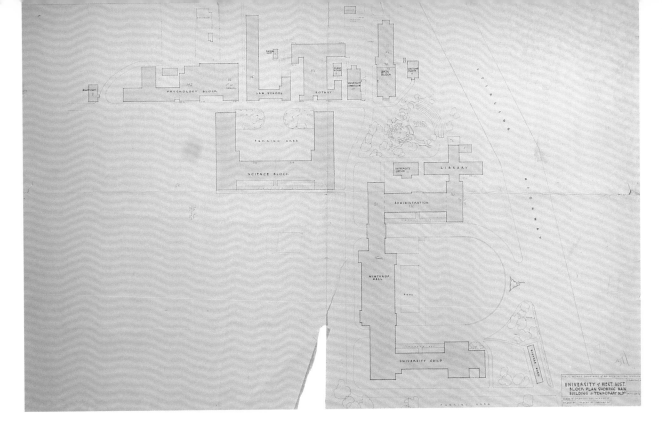

Hackett and Irwin Street buildings,
Public Works Department, 1952

Engineering and Agriculture buildings,
Public Works Department, 1952

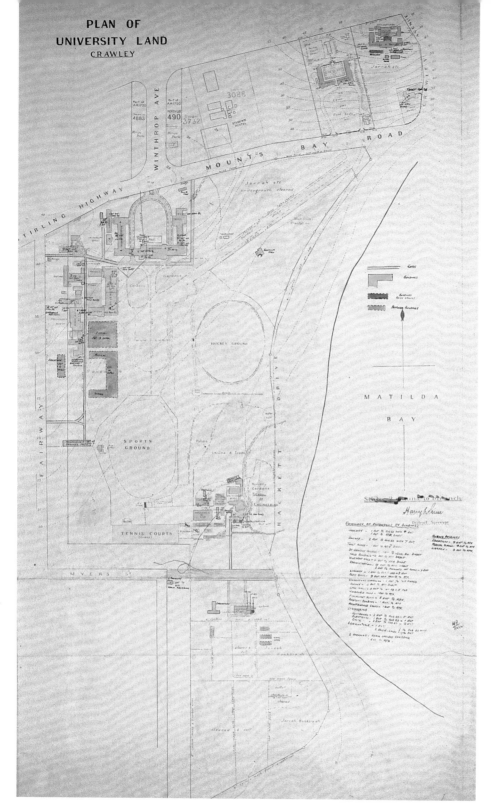

PLAN OF
UNIVERSITY LAND
CRAWLEY

*Future buildings laid over District
Surveyor's 1941 plan, K.V. Benwell,
1952*

DOLA
Department of LAND ADMINISTRATION

Plan of grounds, K.V. Benwell, 1952

GORDON STEPHENSON 1954-55 PLAN

Leslie Wilkinson's 1927 plan had established the spine of the campus, with the three major green spaces, the Great Hall and an element which became the Reid Library on a strong north-south axis. The concentration of buildings shown west of this axis did not accommodate small-scale development or expansion by stages, and by 1952 the area west of the Physics and Chemistry building was occupied by a group of 'temporary' buildings from Irwin Street. Shenton House and Engineering Hall were surrounded on the north, west and south by a village of timber-framed structures, and remnants from the United States Navy's presence on campus flanked the Institute of Agriculture building.

Wilkinson's plan may have adequately served a modest population of around 3,000 students, but by 1952 the University found itself faced with a rapid expansion in population and in 1954 it was assumed that student numbers would reach 7,000 by 1984. It was generally agreed that the University should be planned for a minimum of 8,000 students.[1]

Professor (later Sir) Noel Bayliss, in his capacity as Acting Vice-Chancellor between Dr Currie's resignation in mid-1952 and the arrival of the third permanent Vice-Chancellor Mr (later Sir) Stanley Prescott early in 1953, recognized the deficiencies of the Wilkinson plan and recommended to the University that a suitably qualified person be found to assist the Senate subcommittee on long-range planning.

Bayliss had met and discussed the University's planning problems with Gordon Stephenson who, then Professor of Civic Design at the University of Liverpool, was visiting Perth in his capacity as town planning consultant to the State Government. During the war, he worked as a senior planner in the Ministry of Town and Country Planning in Britain and, when at the University of Liverpool, had acted as adviser to the Dublin University College.[2]

The resiting of the Physics and Chemistry building had been a major departure from the Wilkinson plan, and although Wilkinson was still available for consultation and there was some reluctance to make further departures from the plan, the Senate, early in 1953, agreed to invite Stephenson to attend a meeting of the newly formed Buildings Committee.[3]

This led to Stephenson being commissioned to spend a month as consultant to the University during his second visit to Perth as planning consultant to the State Government. At a special meeting on 31 May 1954, the Senate adopted a plan which had been prepared by Stephenson working closely with the Vice-Chancellor, Stanley Prescott, and from estimates prepared by the Registrar, Dr C. Sanders, for an anticipated student enrolment of 4,750 in 1973 and a required 116,000 square metres of building area for a population of 8,000 students by the late 1980s.[4]

By this time, Stephenson had accepted an appointment as foundation Professor of Town and Regional Planning at the University of Toronto, Ontario, Canada.

The 1954 plan, refined in 1955, retained the basic spinal structure of the Wilkinson plan but dispersed building sites over the whole campus, creating a simple, ordered, but flexible and highly aesthetic arrangement of buildings and spaces. The principles of the plan were that departments were located in functional groups; vehicles were excluded from the inner courts and green spaces; and provisions were made for car parking space. The plan showed parking for 1,000 vehicles. Stephenson recommended against the forced continuation of the Alsop-Sayce style of architecture, although he was a great advocate of all future buildings being in context with the original development.

The plan maintained Wilkinson's 'Alley' as Battye Avenue and relocated the main Library to a central site between the Great Court and James Oval. The Faculty of Education and a teachers training college were located at the southern end of the campus, and residential accommodation was shown on the Women's Hockey Ground on the north-west intersection of Stirling Highway and Hampden Road.

The 1954-55 plan assumed the demolition of Shenton House and Engineering Hall. Myers Street was shown crossing the campus to link with Hackett Drive.

REFERENCES

1. F. Alexander, *Campus at Crawley*, p. 602.
2. G. Stephenson, *On a Human Scale. A Life in City Design*, jacket notes.
3. *Senate Minutes*, 16 March 1953.
4. R.J. Ferguson & Associates, *Campus Planning Review 1990*, p. 17.

Aerial perspective of campus, 1947

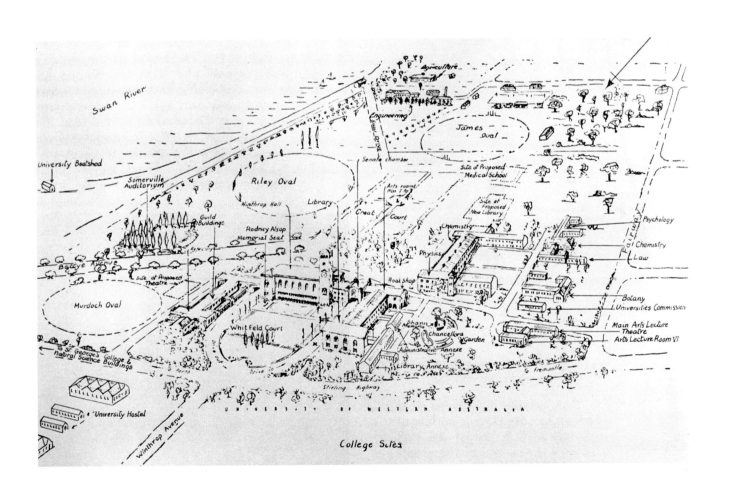

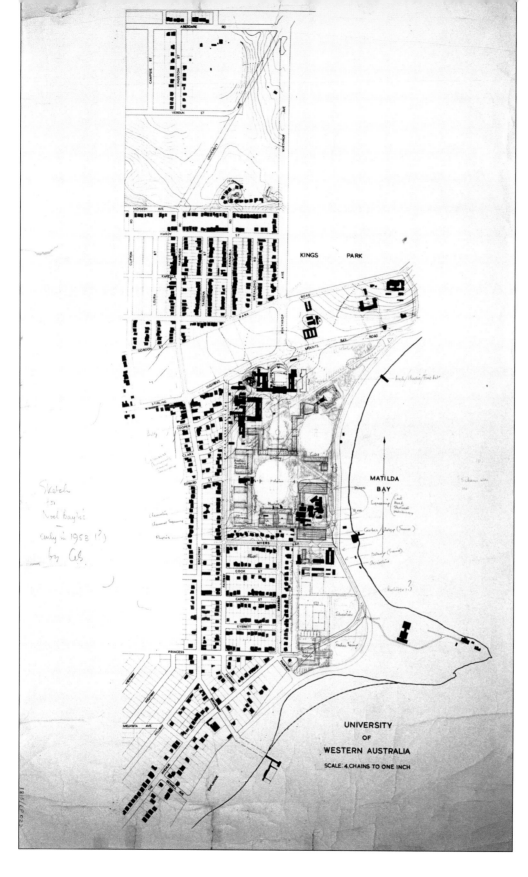

Stephenson campus plan, 1953

Stephenson campus plan, 1954

Stephenson campus
plan, 1955, based on
plan approved by the
Senate in 1954

Additional
Staffhouses
north of
this plan

St George's

St Thomas
More

Projected Colleges

Winthrop

Tuart
House

Mounts   Bay   Road

Stirling   Highway

Admin

Murdoch
Oval

Battye

Avenue

Whitfeld
Court

Guild

Chapel

Irwin
Street

Winthrop
Hall

Fine Arts

Cooper
Street

Great
Court

Riley
Oval

Note in 1954
this area was
occupied by
temporary
buildings on
Irwin Street

Physics

Arts

Library

Social
Science

M   A   T   I   L   D   A

Fairway

James
Oval

Hackett   Drive

B   A   Y

Engineering

Chemistry

Position of Crawley
House and temporary
Engineering buildings 1954

Biological
Sciences

Staff Houses

Myers   Street

Agriculture

Parkway

Zoology

Proposed   Disposition
of Main Elements
Crawley Campus.

Gordon Stephenson
Architect & Planning Consultant

June 1955 based on Plan approved in 1954.

Staff Houses

Faculty of Education

North

Teachers
Training College

50 0   150 300 450 600 750 900   ft.

74

PUBLIC WORKS DEPARTMENT

By 1953, the Principal Architect, Public Works Department, had made extensions to the southern leg of the Alsop-Sayce Administration building and in 1955 had commenced designs of the buildings for Engineering and Biochemistry, these buildings being completed in 1959 and 1960.

Dissatisfaction with the performance of the Public Works Department developed into continuous debates on the merits of competitions and private, local, overseas or government architects for architectural commissions on the campus, especially as the University was on the threshold of a building boom.[1]

In 1958, after much deliberation and political intervention, the Senate decided that Marshall Clifton, a local private architect, and the Principal Architect, Public Works Department, should be invited to collaborate in the preparation and submission to the Senate of preliminary comprehensive sketch plans of the new Chemistry, Physics, Library and Arts buildings.[2]

The Public Works Department proceeded with the documentation and building of the first-stage Chemistry and Physics buildings, both being completed in 1962 on sites in general accord with the 1954-55 Stephenson plan.

In pursuing designs for the Library and Arts buildings, the Principal Architect took it upon himself to review the campus plan, illustrations of which were presented to meetings of the Buildings Committee on 14 and 19 May 1959 with Marshall Clifton's sketch proposals for the buildings. It was explained to the Committee that the building areas required for the Library and Arts buildings could not be met without departing from the quadrilateral framing of the Great Court as depicted in the 1954-55 Stephenson plan and also that it had been 'necessary to consider the integration and harmonizing of the Physics, Chemistry, Engineering, Library, Arts and Hackett buildings'.

The proposal was to relocate James Oval to be adjacent to Hackett Drive and symmetrical with Riley Oval, with a Student Refectory building between the two ovals forming a strong east-west axis with Arts in the centre of the campus. The Library building was moved to a central position in the Great Court and the Arts building was located in the present position of the Reid Library.

Apart from providing additional development space at the expense of the Great Court, the justification for this major departure from the Wilkinson and Stephenson plans was to create identifiable architectural precincts – a 'romantic' group of buildings which included the Hackett Memorial Buildings and the north face of the proposed Library building which was to copy the Winthrop Hall elevation; a 'scientific' group of cheaper construction; and an 'academic' group in which some more expensive materials would be used.

The buildings for the Department of Engineering had been committed and the sketches for Physics and Chemistry had been completed. Presumably these buildings fell in the 'scientific' group.

It was also proposed that the Library, Arts and some unallocated buildings be six storeys in height to help provide 160,000 square metres of building floor area and that parking provision be made for 1,600 vehicles.[3]

The Principal Architect's plan was subsequently presented to the Professorial Board (now the Academic Board) for comment and was not well received. The Vice-Chancellor and Professor Bayliss strongly recommended that Stephenson be invited to review his 1954-55 plan in light of the proposals made by Clifton and the Principal Architect.[4]

The second-stage Engineering buildings, Chemistry and the six-storey Physics building proceeded to completion, but all other proposals of the Principal Architect's plan were set aside by the Senate's decision to invite Stephenson back from Toronto for consultation.

REFERENCES

1. F. Alexander, *Campus at Crawley*, pp. 611-614.
2. *Senate Minutes*, 27 October 1958.
3. Minutes of Buildings Committee meetings, 14 and 19 May 1959.
4. G. Stephenson, *Planning for The University of Western Australia 1914-70*, p. 9.

Campus plan, Public Works Department, 1959

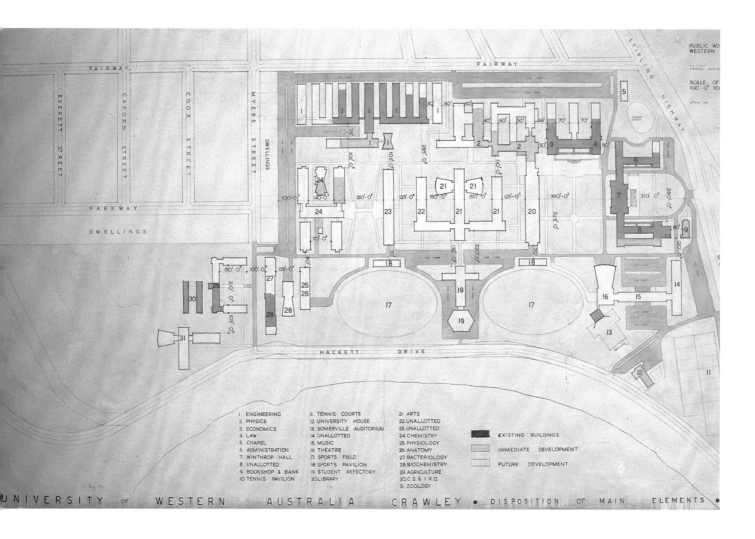

MARSHALL CLIFTON

Marshall Clifton was born in Wokalup, Western Australia, in 1903 and in 1922 began his architectural career, firstly as a Junior Draftsman and then as an Architectural Cadet in the Public Works Department.

He completed his cadetship in 1926 and remained with the Public Works Department as an Assistant Architect until 1929. After completing examinations of the Architects Board of Western Australia, Clifton worked for a short period with architect G. Herbert Parry before travelling to England in 1930. There he studied and worked, with painting excursions to the Continent.

He formed a partnership with Parry in 1933 on his return to Perth, this partnership lasting until 1937 when he set up his own practice. During the Second World War, Clifton joined the Army, attaining the rank of Captain.

In 1946, Clifton and Eric Leach formed a partnership which lasted until 1953, when Leach left Australia for England.

Clifton is best known for his 'Spanish influenced' private houses, his skill and perception as a watercolour artist and his buildings on the Crawley campus. He died in 1975.[1]

Aerial perspective of campus from north, Marshall Clifton, 1959

REFERENCE

1. B. Chapman and D. Richards, *Marshall Clifton Architect and Artist.*

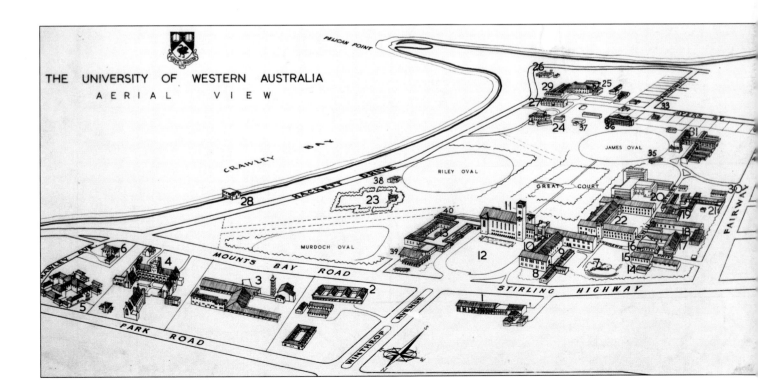

GORDON STEPHENSON 1959-62-65 PLANS

In September 1959, Stephenson spent three weeks at the University reviewing the 1955 plan to accommodate estimated long-term space requirements. These requirements had been prepared by a subcommittee of the Buildings Committee, of which the convenor and executive officer was Dr R.L. Kirk.

The 1959 plan maintained the structure of the 1954-55 plan but intensified the site coverage of buildings, almost to the exclusion of large landscaped spaces, in order to meet the Kirk subcommittee's estimate that 148,000 square metres of space would be required to accommodate students predicted to be enrolled as early as 1967.[1]

In presenting this plan to meetings of the Professorial Board on 10 September 1959 and of the Senate on 24 September 1959, Stephenson reiterated the basic planning principles of the 1954-55 plan, adding that it was undesirable to make provision in buildings for undergraduate classes beyond the third floor but, if necessary, space beyond the third floor – up to six or eight floors – could accommodate such facilities as staff offices and research laboratories. He adhered to his 1955 plan showing the Library in a central location between the Great Court and James Oval, as this building would be 'a dominant next in importance to Winthrop Hall'.

In terms of the design of buildings, Stephenson observed that there were two kinds of designs – good and bad – and that, simply, the University should insist on good designs. He felt that

> all the buildings designed by Alsop should be given respect as, whatever their faults, they were unmistakably 'University' in character and this was a quality very rarely achieved. There must be architecture which had true University character. To achieve this the Architect and the University must together seek the best kinds of solutions in University terms. For the remainder, success would depend on the work being done by a sensitive architect.

The 1959 plan proposed the retention of Whitfeld and Great Courts, James Oval and Somerville Auditorium but nominated a reduction in size of Riley Oval. Stephenson suggested that 'the Shenton Park land was the obvious place for playing fields', emphasized a real need for landscaping on the western side of the campus, and suggested the removal of car parking on the Fairway road verge. The plan made provision for 1,800 parked vehicles.

In accordance with recommendations of the Kirk subcommittee, the teachers training college, located in the southern campus in the 1954-55 plan, was relocated to the site on the north-west corner of the intersection of Hampden Road and Stirling Highway where the Nedlands College was eventually constructed. The Myers Street cross-campus link was deleted on the 1959 plan and Stephenson proposed that the cottages built on sites flanking Myers Street and Parkway could eventually be demolished to provide additional building space.[2] The 1959 plan showed the retention of Shenton House, used possibly as a staff house, a site for which was also shown to the south of Somerville Auditorium at the present location of University House.[3]

Late in 1959, an architectural competition was conducted for the design of a Staff Club on the site south of Somerville Auditorium. Results were announced early in 1960, but the winning design by Perth architect Raymond Jones was not well received by the University House Committee nor by the Buildings Committee nor by the Senate, the design slavishly copying details of the Alsop-Sayce buildings. The competition was considered to be unsuccessful and the building design was totally modified to a 'more modest structure'. University House was completed and opened in 1962.[4]

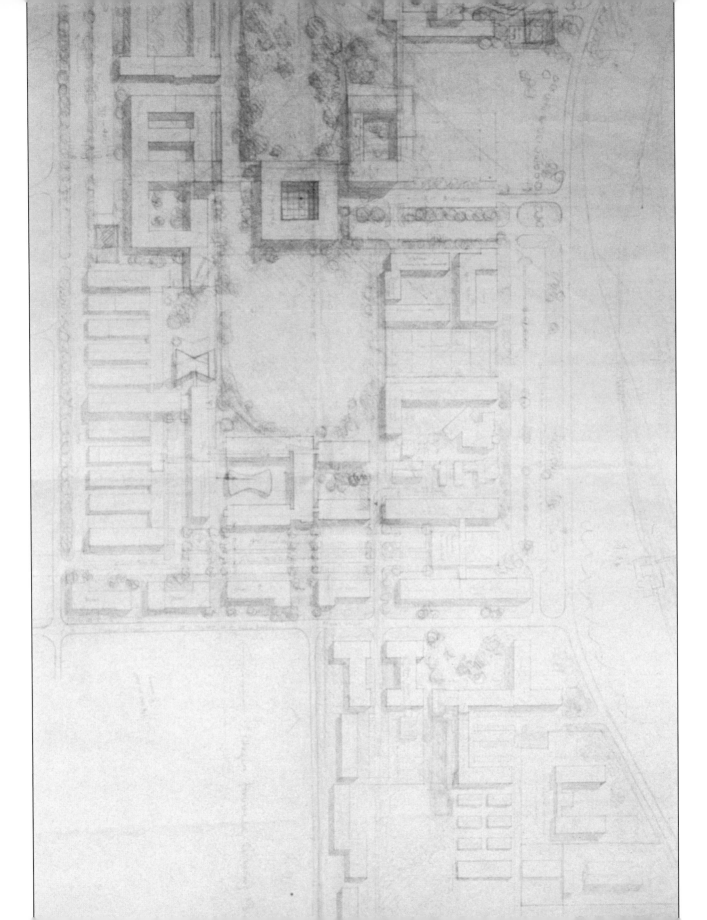

While in Perth to present the 1959 plan, Stephenson accepted an offer to return as permanent Consultant Architect to the University and took up that appointment in 1960, by which time the designs for University House and the Engineering, Chemistry, Biochemistry and Physics buildings had been committed. Stephenson proposed the use of cream (buff) brick for the Physics building and other buildings 'on the west flank of the Great Court'.[5]

This led to buildings for Mathematics, Electrical Engineering, Computing Science and new Electrical Engineering being constructed in clay brick, creating a group of buildings of a notably different surface texture to that of the original limestone and more recent concrete block buildings.

Marshall Clifton completed the eastward extension of Hackett Hall in 1961 and the University Bookshop extension to the north in 1962.

Stephenson reviewed the campus plan in 1962 and again in 1965, the 1965 plan showing even more intense development of the campus than the 1959 and 1962 versions. The 1965 plan was not endorsed by the Senate.

During the period between 1960, when Stephenson assumed his role as Consultant Architect, and 1969, when he resigned this position, he worked in association with several private architects on campus buildings. His role as Consultant Architect to the University and associate design architect to the commissioned project architects ensured that his aims for the physical development of the campus were achieved. The first commissions under this new control system involved Marshall Clifton on the Arts, and Economics and Commerce buildings completed in 1963 and 1966; Cameron Chisholm & Nicol on the Reid Library building completed in 1964; and R.J. Ferguson on the Law School building completed in 1967.

REFERENCES

1. Dr R.J. Kirk, Subcommittee Report, 21 August 1959.
2. Minutes of meetings of the Professorial Board, 10 September 1959, and the Senate, 24 September 1959.
3. ibid.
4. F. Alexander, *Campus at Crawley*, pp. 616-617.
5. Minutes of meetings of the Professorial Board, 10 September 1959, and the Senate, 24 September 1959.

Stephenson campus plan based on plans approved by the Senate in 1959 and 1962

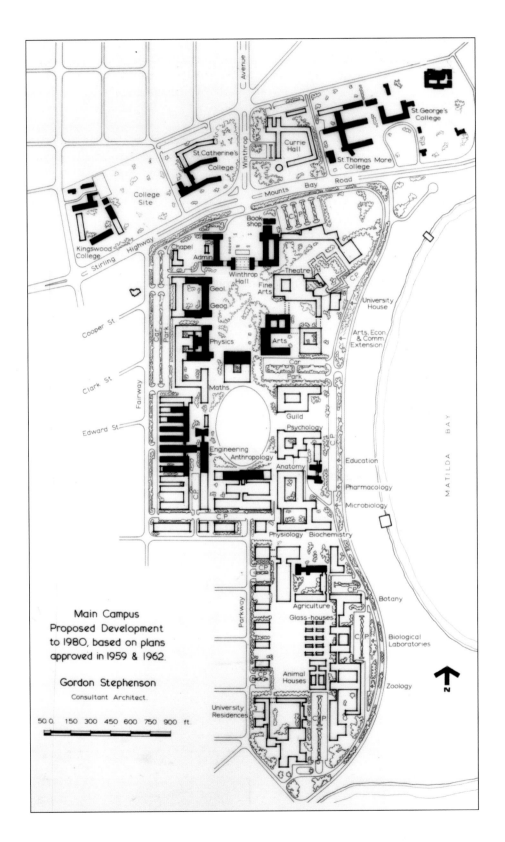

St George's College

St Catherine's College

Currie Hall

St Thomas More College

College Site

Kingswood College

Stirling Highway

Winthrop

C Avenue

Mounts Bay Road

Book shop

Chapel

Admin

Geol

Geog

Winthrop Hall

Theatre

Fine Arts

University House

Arts, Econ & Comm Extension

Cooper St

Physics

Arts

Car Park

Clark St

Maths

Guild

Psychology

Fairway

Edward St

Engineering

Anthropology

Anatomy

Education

Pharmacology

Microbiology

MATILDA BAY

Physiology

Biochemistry

Main Campus
Proposed Development
to 1980, based on plans
approved in 1959 & 1962.

Gordon Stephenson
Consultant Architect.

50 0.   150 300 450 600 750 900 ft.

Parkway

Agriculture

Glass-houses

Botany

Biological Laboratories

Animal Houses

Zoology

University Residences

N

81

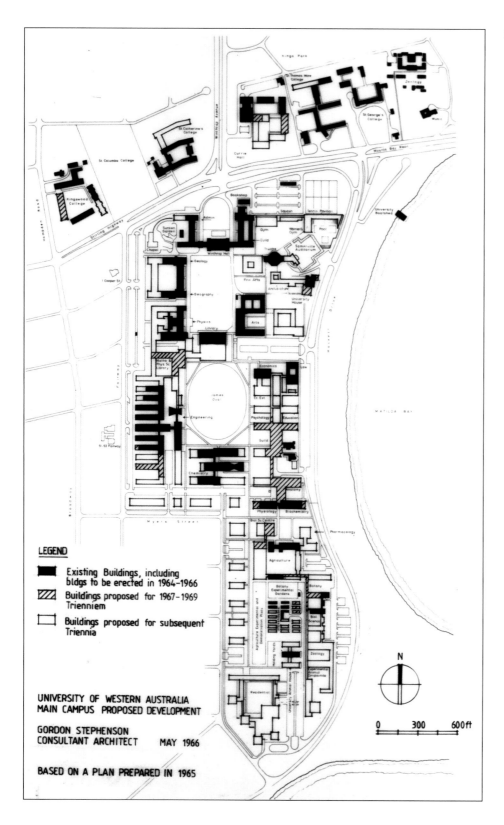

Stephenson campus plan, 1965

LEGEND

■ Existing Buildings, including bldgs to be erected in 1964-1966

▨ Buildings proposed for 1967-1969 Trienniem

☐ Buildings proposed for subsequent Triennia

UNIVERSITY OF WESTERN AUSTRALIA
MAIN CAMPUS PROPOSED DEVELOPMENT

GORDON STEPHENSON
CONSULTANT ARCHITECT   MAY 1966

BASED ON A PLAN PREPARED IN 1965

0   300   600 ft

Arthur Bunbury 1975 Plan

Stephenson was succeeded as Consultant Architect by Arthur Bunbury as University Architect. Bunbury qualified from Melbourne University, then practised as an architect in Melbourne in the partnership Earle and Bunbury and later as Arthur Bunbury and Associates. The practice was appointed Consultant Town Planners to the Shire of Lillydale in 1956. In 1962, Bunbury was appointed Senior Lecturer at the Kuala Lumpur Technical College and then Head of the Architecture Department at the College, completing his assignment in 1964.

When Bunbury arrived at The University of Western Australia late in 1966, buildings had been completed for the first-stage Animal House, Currie Hall, Soil Science, the Administration extension and first-stage Physiology. The Botany and Biology building, Octagon Theatre and Guild Indoor Sports Centre were under construction and the Anatomy and Guild buildings were in the planning stage. The two pedestrian underpasses connecting the main campus with the Currie Hall and St Catherine's College sites were constructed at the time of the 1966 roadworks which were to provide twin carriageways for Stirling Highway and Mounts Bay Road. The underpasses were opened in 1970.

The 1962 Stephenson plan and its revision in 1965 had set the planning structure for the whole campus. All available space was shown utilized for building development to the point where the campus was in danger of losing much of its open landscaped qualities. Buildings were shown covering prime open spaces such as Riley Oval and what is now known as Oak Lawn, and little was left of what became Prescott Court. No other major landscaped spaces were proposed for the southern campus.

In siting buildings for the second-stage Animal House in 1970, Mathematics and the Mathematics and Physical Sciences Library in 1971, Reid Library expansion in 1972, and Social Sciences and Electrical and Electronic Engineering in 1975, Bunbury followed the intent of the Stephenson plan. However, Psychology (1974) was moved further south to be adjacent to Anatomy, and Music (1975), which had been displaced from the 1962 plan by the Guild Recreation Centre and not relocated in the 1965 plan, was located at the eastern end of Somerville Auditorium on a site allocated for Law in the 1962 plan.

The Dolphin Theatre (1976), previously accommodated in temporary buildings adjacent to Shenton House, was located by Bunbury to be adjacent to the Octagon Theatre and with the same orientation as Somerville Auditorium and Music. The space bounded by Hackett Hall, the Recreation Centre and its several extensions, and the Octagon and Dolphin Theatres became informally known as Theatre Court until relandscaped in 1989 and named Lawrence Jackson Court after Sir Lawrence Jackson, Chancellor from 1968 to 1981. This court has become one of the finer spaces on campus and complements the theatres and auditorium.

In 1973, Bunbury prepared an 'Interim Report on Campus Planning with Special Reference to Possible Developments in the 1976-78 Triennium'. The report also made recommendations on the classification of Permanent Green Reserves.

In 1975, Bunbury's 'Report on Campus Planning' superseded the interim report and remained the last formal review of the campus plan until the *Campus Planning Review 1990* prepared by R.J. Ferguson & Associates.

Neither the 1975 nor the 1990 campus planning reviews found reason to depart from the established Stephenson planning principles.

Bunbury's 1975 plan relocated Architecture to the southern campus adjacent to Agriculture, freeing the space around the Octagon Theatre and consequently Riley Oval. Although following the Stephenson pattern of development on Riley Oval, Bunbury proposed a much wider view path across the oval. Later in 1985, Bunbury relocated the new Architecture building to a site immediately east of the Geology and Geography building and north of the General Purpose building, where it was constructed in 1987.

In relocating Psychology further south and Education and Physical Education to the southern campus, more of the Oak Lawn was retained, but even in the 1975 plan the proposed southern duplication of the 350 seat Social Sciences Lecture Theatre reduced the lawn to a token strip. Fortunately, it was found that a second large theatre was not required in that vicinity and the boundaries of Oak Lawn were contained by the southern expansion of Law in 1986, the eastern face of Social Sciences and the northern face of the Guild building. Physical Education became Human Movement and Recreational Studies and was relocated to the extreme south-western corner of the campus, displacing Stephenson's residential building. The first-stage building was completed in 1984 and included a 6,000 square metre grassed Outdoor Laboratory.

After the closure of the cross-campus leg of Myers Street around 1971-72, the road reserve was acquired by the University, but at the time of the 1975 report the road surface remained and was used as an internal campus road joining the Hackett Drive ring road and Chemistry ring road. Bunbury recommended that the road surface be removed and, by restricting the plan form of the proposed new Biological Sciences Library building, the open space to the north of Agriculture gained more prominence. It was landscaped in 1983 and became Prescott Court.

Bunbury secured additional Permanent Green Reserves and located the Child Study Centre on Fairway, completed in 1974; two General Purpose Buildings, the first on Myers Street completed in 1980 and the second immediately west of Geography completed in 1982; the restored and rebuilt Irwin Street Building on the west side of James Oval, completed in 1987; and a Child Care Centre on Parkway, completed in 1988. He also pursued the acquisition of properties off campus between Fairway, Parkway and Broadway for the purpose of expansion of the campus with University/community related projects. This led to the construction of the Edwards Street building completed in 1990 to accommodate the Geomechanics Division of the Commonwealth Scientific and Industrial Research Organisation and others on an off-campus site, including that originally occupied by Anthropology.

At the time of the 1975 report, the realignment of Hackett Drive was in the design stage. The campus was cut by Hackett Drive, and although the realignment shown in the report was not totally achieved, the final location at least resulted in the campus being unified. Between 1979 and 1981, Hackett Drive was joined to be continuous with Princess Road instead of running further south as shown in the Stephenson 1965 plan and the Bunbury 1975 plan. As a result of the dangerous intersection of The Avenue, Princess Road and Hackett Drive, Parkway was closed in 1977, causing some traffic exit problems for the campus.

The 1965 Stephenson plan made provision for 1,900 vehicle parking spaces and Stephenson's recommendation was to limit spaces on campus to 2,000. In the

Bunbury campus plan,
1975

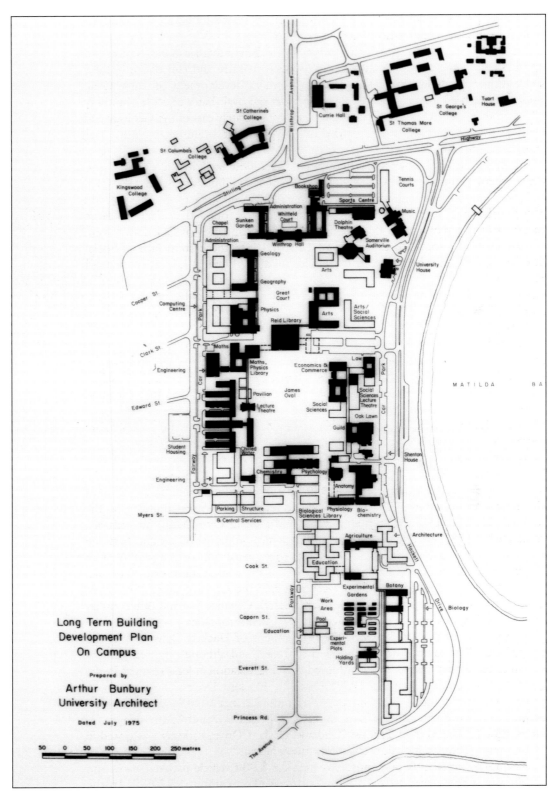

Long Term Building
Development Plan
On Campus

Prepared by

Arthur Bunbury
University Architect

Dated July 1975

presentation of the 1959 plan, it was noted that the student population of the campus should be limited to 9,000. Later, in 1975, Bunbury prepared a document entitled 'Recommendations to the Senate on Parking and Traffic' which predicted a need for 4,000 vehicle spaces for a planned maximum population of 12,000 students. Two thousand of these spaces were to be on or immediately adjacent to campus, employing no more than 10 per cent of the campus at ground level, and the remainder off-campus in adjacent or remote parks possibly served by shuttle buses.

Bunbury also predicted that local authority action would restrict the number of vehicles which could be parked in kerbside situations off-campus, and in 1981 decisions were taken to require the University to make submissions to the then Metropolitan Region Planning Authority (now the Department of Planning and Urban Development), through the City of Subiaco and City of Perth, for development approval for building projects. As predicted, the local authorities have taken this opportunity to require, as part of the approval process, additional parking facilities on campus in order to remove parked University vehicles from the neighbouring streets.

In 1985, on behalf of the University, Bunbury commissioned a 'Traffic and Parking Strategy' by external consultants Feilman Planning Consultants Pty Ltd and Scott and Furphy Engineers Pty Ltd. The final version of this strategy was received in 1986.

Bunbury retired from the position of University Architect late in 1985, and since that date the University has been taking advice from an external Consultant Architect, R.J. Ferguson & Associates.

Arthur Bunbury died on 24 October 1990.

REFERENCE

The above details were taken from various files and plan records held by the University's Property Services Office.

Development Plan, 1990,
R.J. Ferguson &
Associates

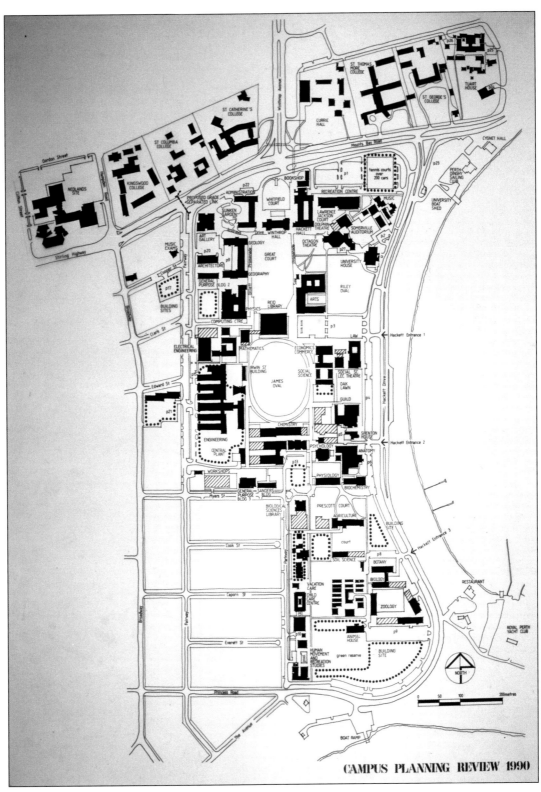

CAMPUS PLANNING REVIEW 1990

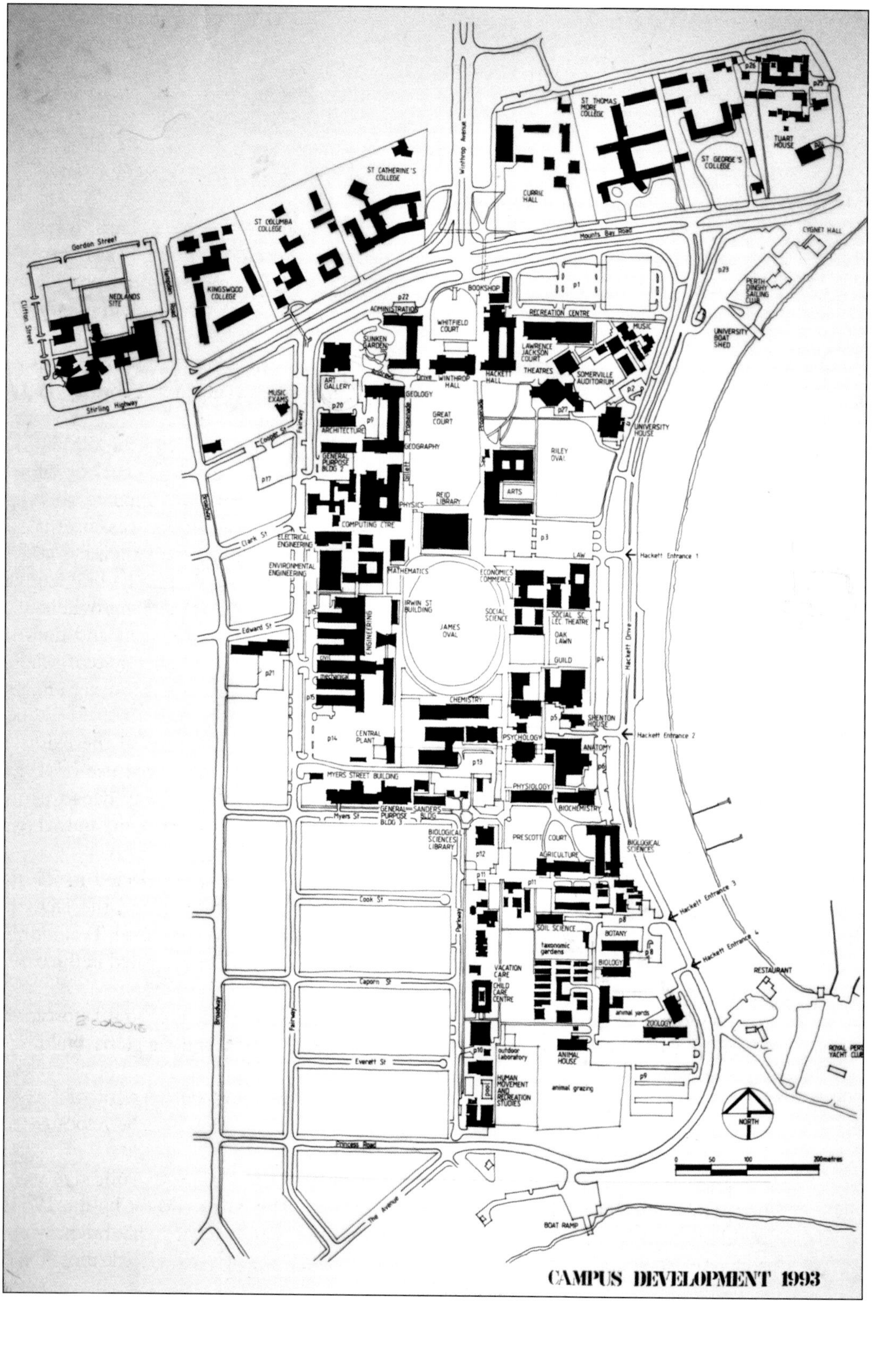

*Campus development, 1993,
R.J. Ferguson &
Associates*

CAMPUS DEVELOPMENT 1993

NEDLANDS SITE

As part of a major building works package financed jointly by the University and the Commonwealth Tertiary Education Commission, negotiations commenced in 1987 for the University to purchase the 3.5 hectare Nedlands campus of the Western Australian College of Advanced Education (WACAE). Nedlands College was constructed in 1967 on the site of the former University Women's Hockey Ground on the corner of Stirling Highway and Hampden Road.

It was noted during negotiations that the Nedlands campus buildings, totalling 14,600 square metres in gross floor area, would eventually require replacement but until then, in conjunction with facilities on the Crawley campus, would provide an expansion potential for some 1,500 students and relieve pressure on accommodation in existing buildings on the Crawley campus.

New facilities for the Nedlands College were constructed at the Mount Lawley campus of WACAE (Edith Cowan University), and were occupied in February 1991, making the Nedlands campus available to the University at that time.

Facilities on the Nedlands site included a five-level Administration/Teaching building and a two-level Teaching/Resource building, the lowest level of which is mostly below ground level. The structure of this building was designed to carry a future two-level vertical extension. An Industrial Arts building was integrated with a one-, two- and three-level Gymnasium building. Other single-level facilities included a Music building, a Student Association building and a Cafeteria building. A 140 seat Lecture Theatre was integrated with the Administration/Teaching building.

Because of the spread of buildings, tennis court, cricket practice nets and hockey field, the campus was not endowed with the open landscaped court system of the Crawley campus. Car parking was mostly contained on the northern and western flanks of the campus.

A study prepared by R.J. Ferguson & Associates in 1991 analysed the existing facilities of the Nedlands site and investigated various options for the use of those facilities. The purpose of the study was to determine which University departments might be suitable tenants for the Nedlands site, if only in the short term, and whose vacation of facilities on the Crawley campus would best benefit that campus.

The School of Architecture and Department of Fine Arts were selected to jointly occupy the refurbished five-level Administration/Teaching building and the Department of Education and Library to occupy the refurbished two-level Teaching/Resource building with a new two-level extension, the Library being located in the basement of the building.

The Gymnasium building was demolished to make way for a central landscaped court, and the Lecture Theatre, Music, Student Association and Cafeteria buildings were refurbished for general purpose use.

University Extension from the Crawley campus and the Department of Public Health from the Queen Elizabeth II Medical Centre were chosen to be relocated to occupy the refurbished two-level Industrial Arts building.

The architectural character and construction of the Nedlands buildings were noticeably different to those of the Crawley campus. The image was set by the 1960s buildings which employed flat concrete roofs, chocolate coloured clay brick, white concrete block and painted Tyrolean render external walling, with black mosaic tile cladding to an exposed structural frame.

Funding would not permit replacement of the external cladding materials with those of the Crawley campus. The flat roofs, most of which allowed the penetration of stormwater and solar heat, were covered with pitched metal roofs. New structural elements were constructed in white concrete to be in harmony with the white concrete blocks and cream Tyrolean rendering in an attempt to unite the various elements of the campus and establish its own positive architectural character in line with that of the Crawley campus but employing different materials and colour scheme.

The site was planned to accommodate future development.

REFERENCE

The above details were taken from a redevelopment report prepared by R.J. Ferguson & Associates in May 1991: *The University of Western Australia, Nedlands Campus, Proposed Redevelopment.*

North elevation, Nedlands campus of WACAE, 1990 (top), and north elevation, redeveloped campus, R.J. Ferguson & Associates, 1993

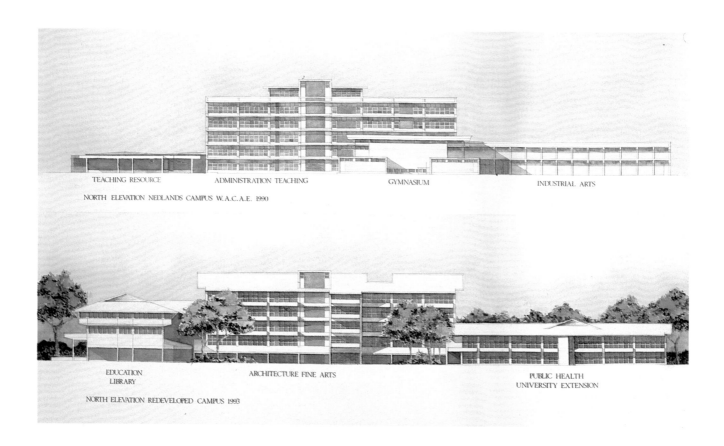

TEACHING RESOURCE   ADMINISTRATION TEACHING   GYMNASIUM   INDUSTRIAL ARTS

NORTH ELEVATION NEDLANDS CAMPUS W.A.C.A.E. 1990

EDUCATION LIBRARY   ARCHITECTURE FINE ARTS   PUBLIC HEALTH UNIVERSITY EXTENSION

NORTH ELEVATION REDEVELOPED CAMPUS 1993

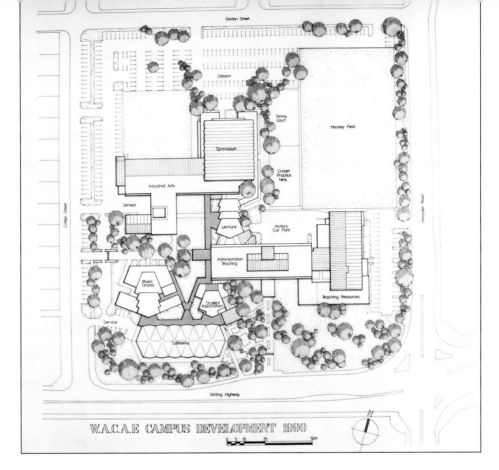

WACAE, campus development, 1990, R.J. Ferguson & Associates

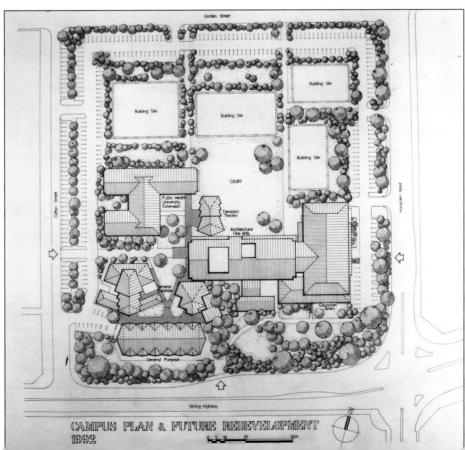

Campus plan and future redevelopment, R.J. Ferguson & Associates, 1992

THE CAMPUS AND ITS EXTENSIONS

The Crawley campus of The University of Western Australia enjoys a location 5 kilometres west of the Perth city centre on the main highway between Perth and Fremantle, close to the centre of gravity of the Metropolitan Region on the banks of the Swan River.

The campus proper covers an area of 46.2 hectares bounded by Mounts Bay Road, Hackett Drive, Parkway, Myers Street, Fairway and Stirling Highway. The extended campus includes an area of 0.72 hectares to the south-east of the intersection of Hackett Drive and Mounts Bay Road and used for car parking; an area of 12.75 hectares to the north of Stirling Highway and Mounts Bay Road and bisected by Winthrop Avenue, which accommodates residential colleges; an additional total area of 0.96 hectares in two lots flanking Winthrop Avenue adjacent to St Catherine's College and Currie Hall; a 2.29 hectare site, the home of Zoology until 1993 and Tuart House; and the recently acquired Nedlands campus of WACAE (Edith Cowan University) on a 3.5 hectare site west of Hampden Road.

The University owns properties off-campus between Fairway, Parkway and Broadway, some of which are occupied by University-related activities.

The Queen Elizabeth II Medical Centre, constructed on 30 hectares of University land, is located less than a kilometre north of the main campus on Winthrop Avenue and accommodates the major part of the Faculty of Medicine, Sir Charles Gairdner Hospital, State Health Laboratories Services and State X-ray Laboratories. The Medical Centre is partly within the City of Subiaco and partly within the City of Nedlands.

Prior to the construction of the Medical Centre, the bulk of teaching in clinical medicine and surgery was conducted at the Royal Perth Hospital, with specialized units at the King Edward Memorial and Princess Margaret Hospitals and small satellite units at the Sir Charles Gairdner Hospital.[1]

University sporting fields, with some service and storage facilities, are accommodated with the 'Superdrome', which provides indoor sporting facilities, on the 50.7 hectare UWA Sports Park at Shenton Park, approximately 3 kilometres from the Crawley campus, between Stephenson Avenue and Brockway Road.

Immediately adjacent to the UWA Sports Park, between Brockway Road and Selby Street, is the 62 hectare Shenton Park campus which has been considered for a Research Campus and accommodates support facilities for the Crawley campus Departments of Agriculture, Botany, Engineering and Zoology.

The Dental School is located in the Perth Dental Hospital buildings in the Perth city centre adjacent to the Royal Perth Hospital.

The Claremont Community Health Centre, owned by the University and located on Stirling Highway at Freshwater Parade, provides facilities for the Department of General Practice, the West Australian Centre for Remote Rural Medicine, Community Health Research and Training, teaching and student areas, and facilities for community groups such as Community District Nurse, Child Health Nurse and Main Hall for general community functions.

Other tenants include general practitioners, a speech therapist, a physiotherapist, the Royal Australian College of General Practitioners, the Family Medical Clinic, the Family Medicine Programme and the After Hours Family Medical Clinic.

Reproduced by permission of the Department of Land Administration, Perth, Western Australia, under Copy Licence 403/93

More distant facilities include the Marine Biology Laboratory at Watermans Bay and the 180 hectare Harry Waring Marsupial Research Station at Jandakot, which provide facilities for Zoology. There are also the 675 hectare Allendale and Hope Valley Farms at Wundowie and the Irrigated Summer Crops Research Centre at Waroona, which provide facilities for the School of Agriculture.

The Crawley campus is located mostly within the City of Subiaco, with a small area in the north-east corner within the City of Perth. The common boundary between the Cities of Subiaco and Nedlands is Broadway and Hampden Road, placing the Nedlands site within the City of Nedlands.

Immediately north of the college sites, east of Winthrop Avenue, is the 417 hectare Kings Park, located on Mount Eliza, controlled by the Kings Park Board. Kings Park is preserved primarily as natural bushland but with areas accommodating tennis courts, children's playgrounds, botanical gardens, an arboretum, memorials and a restaurant. Some areas are maintained as parkland and others as gardens.

The river foreshore between Mounts Bay Road and the Crawley boat ramps, immediately east of the campus off Hackett Drive, is a Class A Reserve vested in the National Parks and Nature Conservation Authority and controlled by the Department of Conservation and Land Management (CALM). Generally, the area is used for public recreation purposes, and facilities, some leased from CALM, include the Perth Dinghy Sailing Club, University Boat Club, Royal Perth Yacht Club, Matilda Bay Sailing Club, a kiosk and a restaurant. A nature conservation area is maintained as a bird sanctuary on Point Currie, with restricted access.

The University enjoys expansive views to the east and south across the river, and many of the public enjoying the river foreshore areas also access the campus for recreation purposes, using campus facilities, particularly car parks.

The University in the Metropolitan Area, overlaid on Metropolitan Region Scheme Map Number 5 dated 14 November 1986 ▷

REFERENCES

1. E. Saint, 'Medicine', in B. de Garis (ed.), *Campus in the Community*, p. 322.

Other details were taken from the *Campus Planning Review 1990*, prepared by R.J. Ferguson & Associates.

EDITH COWAN UNIVERSITY
CHURCHLANDS

EDITH COWAN UNIVERSITY
MT. LAWLEY

SHENTON PARK
CAMPUS

PERTH CITY

UWA
SPORTS
PARK

KINGS PARK

PERTH
MEDICAL
CENTRE

UNIVERSITY
OF W.A.

EDITH COWAN UNIVERSITY
CLAREMONT

SWAN RIVER

CURTIN
UNIVERS

FREMANTLE

MURDOCH
UNIVERSITY

THE UNIVERSITY IN
THE METROPOLITAN
AREA

CAMPUS ARCHITECTURE

The Hackett Memorial Buildings, comprising Winthrop Hall and the Administration and Guild buildings, responded well to the challenges set by the Wilkinson plan and endowed the campus with a generous palette of pitched terracotta tiled roofs, limestone walls and a variety of colonnades, porches, towers and spaces. The grandeur of their composition and the visual strength of the mass, form and colour of the buildings set a formidable design standard for subsequent building development.

Apart from a few instances, later development has displayed remarkably good manners in seeking to honour the qualities of the original buildings and in diverse ways has achieved a totality of design rare on campuses developed over a period of time under a variety of influences. The achievement is more notable because of the design constraints imposed by the established palette of materials and building elements, which is unforgiving of any major variation.

The architectural success of the campus has been achieved by various buildings, each individual architectural statements in their own right, being designed to be compatible with their neighbours – and particularly with the original group of buildings – through scale, colour and texture, without being constrained in terms of sculptural innovation or choice of materials.

This continuance of character and image is not apparent on most campuses with beginnings similar to those of the Crawley campus. Many other universities support a philosophy of respecting their older buildings as part of the heritage of the campuses but encouraging new buildings to explore the fashions and styles of the particular times in which they are constructed. Very few of these campuses enjoy architectural success.

An example of this approach on the Crawley campus is the stylistic expression of the 1960 Engineering library and lecture theatres building, which was fashionable at a time when Brasilia was under construction and when bold mosaic tile patterns were applied to internal and external wall surfaces of buildings, following examples set by Mexico's University City. The buildings, while true to their times and in line with some of their city contemporaries, depart from the campus character and disrupt the totality of the architecture achieved elsewhere on campus. This approach had total University support at the time, as it was thought, correctly, that new buildings should not, and in fact economically could not, ape the Hackett Buildings. However, instead of following a simple contextual design approach, the buildings set out to establish an independent competing image of their own as if oblivious to the architectural strength of the Hackett Buildings

If this free-ranging philosophy had been continued, the campus would now boast a collection of sheer walled buildings clad in mirrored glass, a style which was highly fashionable some years ago despite the moral and legal issues of reflecting one's solar glare and heat onto another's property; and, more recently, 'post modern' buildings reproducing thinly applied elements of the past as 'facadism'; and, currently, buildings expressing something akin to Federation style.

It is notable and not accidental that the group of four buildings – Arts, Reid Library, Economics and Commerce, and Law – constructed immediately after Stephenson's appointment as Consultant Architect, each by a different architect employing different materials and achieving individual identity, form and architectural quality, are compatible with the original buildings and contribute to a continuance of character and image across campus.

The Arts building employed limestone walls, and scaling and detailing reminiscent of elements of the Hackett Buildings. The Reid Library, recipient of the triennial Royal Institute of British Architects Bronze Medal 1964, was clad in exposed aggregate precast concrete panels. The Economics and Commerce building used limestone spandrel panels within an 'off form' concrete structural frame, and the Law School building, recipient of the triennial Royal Australian Institute of Architects Bronze Medal 1969, was constructed with 'off form' concrete load-bearing walls.

The four buildings achieved visual continuity with the Hackett Buildings through their compatible scaling, their terracotta tiled roofs and limestone coloured walls and structure.

Critics of the campus find deficiencies in the simplicity and consistent heights of buildings, the persistence of the terracotta roof tiles, and what appears to be piecemeal development caused by relatively small buildings being sited in isolation from linked neighbours to allow for their own expansion. Others find that when the various buildings are assessed individually, many do not meet the fashion criteria expected of their contemporaries elsewhere in the community. The lesson for the community, and particularly for the city streetscapes, is in the fact that most campus buildings are free from passing fashions and achieve individual merit by contributing to the success of the total campus.

The relatively minor departure from the established image of the limestone scaled wall texture of the Hackett Buildings to that of the imperial sized clay brick, despite colours being compatible, is noticeable and has developed an independent image in the area of Physics, Mathematics, Computing Science and Electrical Engineering on the west side of the campus.

The larger scale and various textures of the limestone wall elements of the Hackett Buildings and some more recent buildings find sympathy with a variety of materials, including large concrete blocks, in situ 'off form' concrete and exposed aggregate precast concrete panels, but not with small imperial size bricks or blocks which have a finite scale and texture of their own.

The painted timber-walled, iron-roofed, reconstructed Irwin Street Building and the stylistic Engineering and Chemistry buildings contribute to a group on the western flank which departs significantly from the campus image.

REFERENCE

The above details were taken from the *Campus Planning Review 1990*, prepared by R.J. Ferguson & Associates.

View of School of Architecture (1987), Geology and Geography buildings (1935)

ILLUSTRATIONS

NEDLANDS SITE

THE CAMPUS AND ITS EXTENSIONS

CAMPUS ARCHITECTURE

CHRONOLOGY

1904	University Endowment Act.
1909	Royal Commission chaired by John Winthrop Hackett to report on the establishment of a university.
1911	University of Western Australia Act.
1912	The first Senate appointed, with John Winthrop Hackett as Chancellor.
1912	Temporary administrative offices rented in Cathedral Avenue, Perth.
1912	Site made available in Irwin Street, Perth, for first temporary accommodation.
1913	Eight foundation chairs established.
1913	First temporary building completed by Public Works Department (PWD) for teaching at Irwin Street.
1914	Crawley site made available for permanent accommodation.
1914	School of Mining and Engineering moved from Irwin Street to occupy the Shenton homestead on the Crawley site.
1914	Competition for the layout of the Crawley site.
1915	Layout competition entries received. Harold Desbrowe-Annear first prize.
1916	Death of Sir John Winthrop Hackett.
1918	St John's Hostel, Perth. Boarding-house for university students.
1920	The University formalized its 999 year lease for the Crawley site with the Crown.
1922	Senate committee appointed to report on buildings required and their location on campus.
1923	Foundation stone of the Biology and Geology building, designed by PWD, laid by Premier James Mitchell.
1925	First permanent University building completed.
1926	Benefits of Hackett bequest became known.
1926	Henry Campbell commenced landscaping the Crawley campus.
1926	University Colleges Act.
1926	Professor Leslie Wilkinson invited to advise on campus planning and also to assist with the competition for the Hackett Memorial Buildings.
1926	Winthrop Hall competition.
1927	Winthrop Hall competition entries received. Rodney H. Alsop and Conrad H. Sayce awarded first prize.
1927	Second permanent building erected by PWD for School of Mining and Engineering, adjacent to Shenton homestead.
1927	Leslie Wilkinson plan for the Crawley campus.
1927	Somerville Auditorium planting completed.
1929	Foundation stones of Winthrop Hall and Hackett Hall laid in presence of Lady (Hackett) Moulden and John Winthrop Hackett junior.
1929	Foundation stone of St George's College laid. Architects Hobbs, Smith and Forbes.
1930	Administration building occupied.
1930	Oliver Dowell appointed as head gardener.
1931	St George's College opened.
1932	Winthrop Hall opened.
1932	The Hackett Memorial Buildings awarded the Royal Institute of British Architects Bronze Medal for excellence in design.
1932	Irwin Street buildings relocated to Crawley campus.
1934	Physics and Chemistry building designs by architects Baxter Cox and Summerhayes approved by the Senate. Construction completed in 1935.
1934	Tuart House, first official residence for the Vice-Chancellor, designed by architects Baxter Cox and Summerhayes.

1936	Memorial to Professor E.O.G. Shann erected in the Sunken Garden.
1938	Institute of Agriculture building, designed by architects Baxter Cox and Leighton, completed in southern campus.
1938	Myers Street extended across campus to link with Hackett Drive.
1938	Programme commenced to construct staff houses in Parkway, Myers Street, Monash Avenue and Arras Street.
1943	United States Navy seaplane base in Matilda Bay. Temporary buildings constructed on campus.
1945	PWD extensions to the Biology and Geology building.
1946	United States Navy Bachelor Officer Quarters converted to student accommodation (the Hostel).
1946	PWD refurbished United States Navy structures and erected new timber-framed buildings adjacent to Shenton House for the School of Engineering.
1953	Professor Gordon Stephenson invited to advise on campus planning.
1953	PWD extensions to the Alsop-Sayce Administration building completed.
1954	Stephenson plan.
1955	St Thomas More College opened.
1959	Architect Marshall Clifton and Principal Architect, PWD, A.E. Clare, presented a revised campus plan with sketch plans of new Chemistry, Physics, Library and Arts buildings.
1959	PWD designed Engineering building completed.
1959	Professor Gordon Stephenson invited to review his 1954-55 campus plan.
1959	Competition for Staff Club building. First prize awarded to architect Raymond Jones.
1959	Stephenson accepted offer to return as permanent Consultant Architect to the University.
1960	PWD designed Biochemistry building completed.
1960	St Catherine's College opened.
1961	Marshall Clifton completed the eastward extension of Hackett Hall.
1962	Clifton completed the University Bookshop extension.
1962	PWD designed Physics and Chemistry buildings completed.
1962	University House opened.
1962	Stephenson reviewed the 1959 campus plan.
1963	Kingswood College opened.
1965	Stephenson reviewed the 1962 campus plan.
1966	Arthur Bunbury appointed as University Architect.
1967	Currie Hall opened.
1967	Stephenson resigned as Consultant Architect to become foundation Professor of the new School of Architecture.
1971	St Columba College opened.
1973	Bunbury Interim Report on Campus Planning.
1975	Bunbury Report on Campus Planning.
1985	Bunbury retired from the position of University Architect.
1986	Traffic and Parking Strategy received.
1987	The University acquired the Nedlands campus of the Western Australian College of Advanced Education.
1990	Campus Planning Review by R.J. Ferguson & Associates.

BIBLIOGRAPHY

GENERAL TEXTS AND ARTICLES

Alexander, F., *Campus at Crawley*, F.W. Cheshire for the University of Western Australia Press, Nedlands, 1963.

Australia's Fighting Sons of the Empire: Portraits and Biographies of Australians in the Great War, Palmer and Ashworth, Melbourne, 1920.

Battye, J.S., *The Cyclopedia of Western Australia*, 2 vols, Hussey and Gillingham Ltd, Adelaide and Perth, 1912-13.

Chapman, B., and Richards, D., *Marshall Clifton Architect and Artist*, Fremantle Arts Centre Press, South Fremantle, 1989.

Freeland, J.M., *Architecture in Australia a History*, F.W. Cheshire Publishing Pty Ltd, Melbourne, 1968.

Robinson, D., *Dove Rising. A Brief History of St Columba College*, St Columba College, Perth, 1980.

Saint, E., 'Medicine', in B. de Garis (ed.), *Campus in the Community: The University of Western Australia, 1963-1987*, University of Western Australia Press, Nedlands, 1988.

Stephens, R., 'A Sweet Spot in an Old Colonial Garden. The Historical Background of the Site of The University of Western Australia', *Journal and Proceedings of the Royal Western Australian Historical Society*, vol. IV, no. 2, Nedlands, 1950

Stephenson, G., *Planning for The University of Western Australia 1914-70*, Langham Press, Nedlands, 1986.

Stephenson, G., *On a Human Scale. A Life in City Design*, Fremantle Arts Centre Press, South Fremantle, 1992.

Stewart, N., *St Catherine's College. From Dream to Reality 1928-1978*, St Catherine's College, Perth, 1978.

Wilkinson, D., *Leslie Wilkinson. A Practical Idealist*, Valadon Publishing, Woollahra, 1982.

Williams, A.E., *Western Australia. An Architectural Heritage*, Williams Pioneer Publications, Perth, 1979.

Williams, A.E., *From Campsite to City*, City of Nedlands, Nedlands, 1984.

OFFICIAL DOCUMENTS, RECORDS AND REPORTS

Alexander, F., 'Collected Papers', University File No. 2424, Battye Library.

'Buildings Committee Meetings', The University of Western Australia.

Convocation Minutes, The University of Western Australia.

Ferguson, R.J., & Associates, *Parliament House Precinct Policy Review*, 1981.

Ferguson, R.J., & Associates, *The University of Western Australia Campus Planning Review 1990*.

Ferguson, R.J., & Associates, *The University of Western Australia, Nedlands Campus, Proposed Redevelopment*, 1991.

Files and Plan Records, The University of Western Australia.

Information, Conditions and Particulars for Guidance in the Preparation of Competitive Designs for the Laying Out of the Grounds and Gardens including the Disposition of the Buildings of The University of Western Australia, Government Printer, 1914.

James, Bill, *Landscape Review*, The University of Western Australia, 1992.

Kirk, Dr R.J., Convenor and Executive Officer, Subcommittee of Buildings Committee, 1959, University Space Requirements Report, The University of Western Australia.

Minute Book, Architectural Competition, The University of Western Australia.

Minute Book, Private, Architectural Competition, The University of Western Australia.

Minutes of Professorial Board, The University of Western Australia.

Opening of Winthrop Hall. Commemoration Volume And Official Programme. April 13 to April 17 1932, The University of Western Australia.

Public Works Department, Plans and Records, State Archives of Western Australia.

Senate Minutes, The University of Western Australia.

Smith, G.G., 'The University Garden', *University Gazette*, 1960.

Winthrop Hall Competition, Assessors' Report, The University of Western Australia, 1927.

UNPUBLISHED PAPERS

Boyce, P.J., 'The Hon. Sir J. Winthrop Hackett, KCMG, Hon. LL.D. His Life and Times', 1955, Battye Library.

Davis, C.E.S., 'St John's University Hostel', Battye Library.

Fraenkel, P.H., 'Reminiscences from the School of Engineering & Mining of The University of Western Australia', a paper presented to the Institution of Engineers, Perth, 1935, Battye Library.

Somerville, W., 'A Blacksmith Looks at a University. The First Thirty Years of the University of Western Australia, being Recollections and Impressions of W. Somerville, LL.D.', 1946, Battye Library.

Somerville, W., 'Somerville Auditorium and its Stage and the Sunken Garden', 1954, The University of Western Australia.

JOURNALS AND NEWSPAPERS

The Architect, Journal of the Royal Australian Institute of Architects (WA Chapter).

Sunday Times, Perth.

West Australian, Perth.

Western Mail, Perth.

TEXT PERMISSIONS

The author has made every effort to secure permission to quote and draw reference from other source material. Despite these efforts, the relatives of some deceased authors have not been able to be traced, and the publisher would welcome any relevant information. Thanks are due to the copyright owners of the following:

Alexander, F.
: *Campus at Crawley*, F.W. Cheshire for the University of Western Australia Press, Nedlands, 1963.

Alsop, H.D.
: Personal notes.

Boyce, P.J.
: 'The Hon. Sir J. Winthrop Hackett KCMG, Hon. LL.D. His Life and Times', 1955, unpublished paper, Battye Library.

Chapman B. and Richards, D.
: *Marshall Clifton Architect and Artist*, Fremantle Arts Centre Press, 1989.

Davis, C.E.S.
: 'St John's University Hostel', unpublished paper, Battye Library.

Fraenkel, P.H.
: 'Reminiscences from the School of Engineering & Mining of The University of Western Australia', a paper presented to the Institution of Engineers, Perth, 1935, unpublished paper, Battye Library.

Freeland, J.M.
: *Architecture in Australia a History*, F.W. Cheshire Publishing Pty Ltd, 1968.

James, W.
: *Landscape Review*, The University of Western Australia, 1992.

Robinson, D.
: *Dove Rising. A Brief History of St Columba College*, St Columba College, 1980.

Saint, E.
: 'Medicine', in *Campus in the Community*, University of Western Australia Press, 1988.

Smith, G.G.
: 'The University Garden' *University Gazette*, 1960.

Somerville, W.   'A Blacksmith Looks at a University. The First Thirty Years of the University of Western Australia, being Recollections and Impressions of W. Somerville, LL.D.', unpublished paper, 1946, Battye Library.

'Somerville Auditorium and its Stage and the Sunken Garden', 1954. The University of Western Australia.

Stephens, R.   'A Sweet Spot in an Old Colonial Garden. The Historical Background of the Site of The University of Western Australia', a paper read to the Royal Western Australian Historical Society, 1950.

Stephenson, G.   *Planning for The University of Western Australia 1914-70*, Langham Press, 1986.

On a Human Scale. A Life in City Design, Fremantle Arts Centre Press, 1992.

Stewart, N.   *St Catherine's College. From Dream to Reality 1928-1978*, St Catherine's College, 1978.

Wilkinson, D.   *Leslie Wilkinson. A Practical Idealist*, Valadon Publishing, 1982.

Williams, A.E.   *Western Australia. An Architectural Heritage*, Williams Pioneer Publications, 1979.

From Campsite to City, City of Nedlands, 1984.

The Architect, Journal of the Royal Australian Institute of Architects (WA Chapter).
Sunday Times, Perth
West Australian, Perth.

INDEX

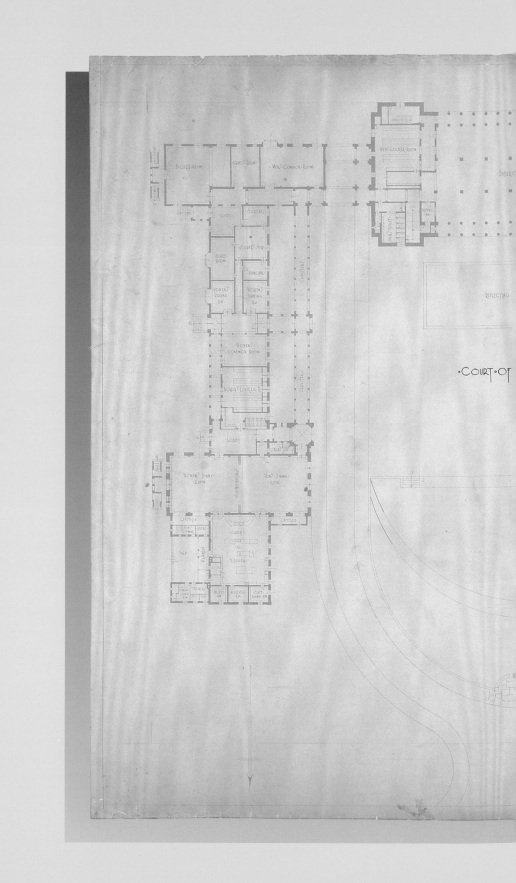

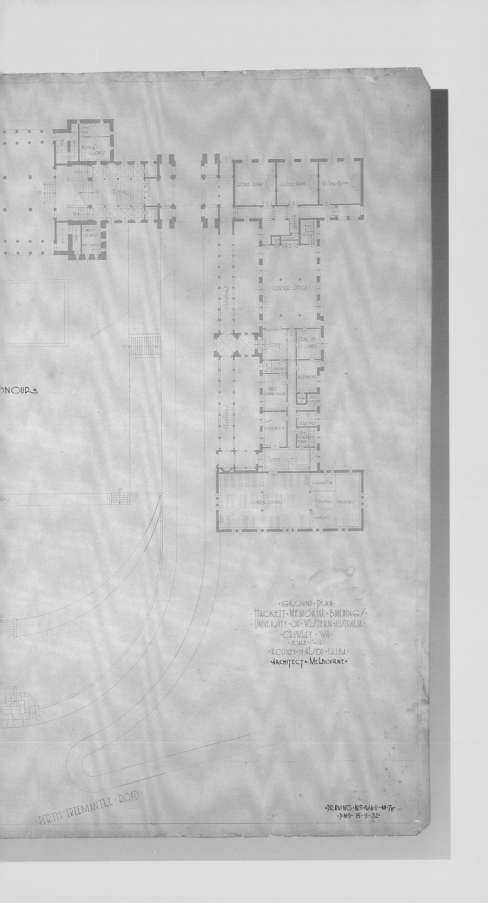

·GROUND·PLAN·
·HACKETT·MEMORIAL·BUILDINGS·
·UNIVERSITY·OF·WESTERN·AUSTRALIA·
·CRAWLEY·WA·
·SCALE·1"=16'·
·RODNEY·H·ALSOP·F·R·I·B·A·
·ARCHITECT·MELBOURNE·

·PERTH·FREEMANTLE·ROAD·

·DRAWING·No·W·A·U·M·76·
·D·M·D·15-9-32·